10-13-64   (64-13720)

The Diary of
Cotton Mather, D.D., F.R.S.
for the Year 1712

1712

The Lth Year.

He Who diligently Seeketh Good Procureth Favour. Paraphrasis Patriciana. "He that from the Time he rises, Studies
nothing but how to Do Good unto others, shall obtain Favour
both with God and Man."

A German some few years Since, one Sebastian Heinric published for the Course of one year, Whatever he Did, Read, or
Saw, every Day in that year. Otium delitiosum, in quo, objecta
vel in Actione, vel in Lectione, vel in Visione, ad Singulos Dies
Anni 1629. Observata representantur. [illegible] of [illegible]

Tully, towards the End of his Book, De Senectute, says; Quod
si, in hoc Erro, quod Animos hominum Immortales esse credam,
Lebenter Erro; nec mihi hunc Errorem, quo delector, dum vivo,
Extorqueri volo.

1712.

The L th Year.

Prov. XI. 27

He who diligently seeketh good procureth favour
paraphrasis perinterarea. He that from the time his
ariseth, studies nothing but how to do good unto others,
he shall obtain favour both with God & man. —

A German found few years since, who had been accustomed
for y~e~ course of one year, whatever he did, heard,
or saw, every day in that year. Diem deliciosum, on
quis, dixerim vel in serious, vel in seriously, vel in actions, etc
singulos dies anni 1629. observation repetat benevolum.

Really towards y~e~ End of his Book, Dr Vincentia serus
tried from his own, quod me thuos Deo mundan junior
rate obe credam, in honour Deo, vel inihi Deum
Erroris, qui debeor dum vivo, extinguere volo.

The Diary of
COTTON MATHER
D.D., F.R.S.
for the Year 1712

Edited with an Introduction and Notes by

WILLIAM R. MANIERRE II
Rutgers, The State University of New Jersey

THE UNIVERSITY PRESS OF VIRGINIA
Charlottesville

Acknowledgments

M Y INDEBTEDNESS exceeds my powers of acknowledgment. The Introduction and Notes do not begin to suggest the largeness of my debt to the host of scholars and critics who have illuminated the early years of America's history. Especially useful have been *Cotton Mather: A Bibliography of His Works,* compiled in three volumes by Thomas James Holmes (Cambridge, Mass., 1940)[1] and *Sibley's Harvard Graduates,* ten volumes (Cambridge, Mass., 1873–1933),[2] by John Langdon Sibley and Clifford K. Shipton. My particular thanks are owed the Massachusetts Historical Society, the American Antiquarian Society, and the Boston Public Library for kindly permitting me to use the Mather materials in their possession. My thanks also to the Rev. John Nicholls Booth for making available to me the records and books of the Second Church in Boston, of which he is presently the minister, and to the Rev. John A. Harrer, Librarian, Congregational Library of the American Congregational Association.

The title page of Cotton Mather's 1712 diary and the four pages of his "printed letter" are reproduced by permission of the Alderman Library, University of Virginia. Without the enthusiastic and friendly assistance of Mr. John Wyllie's staff at the University of Virginia's Alderman Library, with special mention of Miss Helena Koiner, Miss Ann Freudenberg, Miss Katherine Beville, Mr. William Runge, and Mr. Robert Stocking, this edition would not have been possible. As usual in such cases, I take upon myself whatever faults the book exhibits.

[1] Hereinafter referred to as Holmes.
[2] Hereinafter referred to as Sibley.

Table of Contents

LIST OF ILLUSTRATIONS

Introduction

WORTHINGTON CHAUNCEY FORD'S edition of the *Diary of Cotton Mather* has appeared in print twice during the twentieth century: first, in two sizable volumes published in 1911–12 by the Massachusetts Historical Society and, second, in a 1957 reprint of these volumes by the Frederick Ungar Publishing Company. Even before the published version, however, Mather biographers had found indispensable the manuscript diaries available to them in the libraries of three institutions. In 1891, when Barrett Wendell published his *Cotton Mather: The Puritan Priest*, the Massachusetts Historical Society had in its keeping sixteen of Mather's annual diaries, the American Antiquarian Society eight, and the Congregational House one.[1] The location of all other Mather diaries was unknown, their existence seriously doubted. Among these lost manuscripts was that of 1712, for which year Professor Wendell explicitly states, "Mather's diary . . . is not preserved." [2] Still missing in 1911–12, it could not, of course, be included in Ford's edition.

In 1919 it finally turned up at public auction in New York—the first, and so far the last, of Mather's "missing" diaries to be recovered. Here, as lot 213A of Scott-O'Shaughnessy Sale number 62, it was purchased for William Gwynn Mather, whose magnificent

[1] The present distribution is as follows: Massachusetts Historical Society: 1681, 1683, 1685, 1686, 1693, 1697, 1698, 1700, 1701, 1702, 1705, 1706, 1707, 1718, 1721, 1724; American Antiquarian Society: 1688 (a fragment), 1692, 1696, 1699, 1703, 1709, 1711, 1713, 1717; Congregational House: 1716; University of Virginia: 1712.

[2] *Cotton Mather: The Puritan Priest* (London, 1891), p. 238.

collection of Matheriana has subsequently become part of the Tracy W. McGregor Collection of the University of Virginia's Alderman Library. Unfortunately, previous ownership remains an almost complete mystery. McKay's *Book Auction Catalogue* identifies the sale items as coming from the library of "Theodore Brockton De Vinne." *American Book-Prices Current,* however, ascribes them to "Theodore L. De Vinne." I have been unable to discover further evidence of De Vinne ownership. Moreover, since the auction placed on sale unidentified "additions" possessed by unidentified persons, the possibility remains that our diary was never owned by the De Vinnes at all. In short, though I have searched diligently and bothered innumerable persons for information, I have not come up with the expected, scholarly *Eureka;* I have failed to trace ownership back beyond this point.

There exists, however, a tempting lead from the other direction —from past to present—which, though pertinent to this edition and of some interest in itself, has proved equally fruitless as a basis for establishing the history of ownership. The only "available" Cotton Mather diary until now unpublished in this century, the 1712 manuscript is, curiously enough, one of the only two which had received the dignity of publication previous to the date of Ford's collection. Between 1816 and 1820 the staunchly conservative *Panoplist and Missionary Magazine* (Vols. XII–XVI) printed substantial extracts from the diaries of 1712 and 1716. The latter subsequently became the property of the Congregational Library and was included in the Ford edition. But the former, after publication in the *Panoplist,* somehow dropped from sight for a hundred years. So completely did it disappear that nineteenth- and early twentieth-century scholars were not only ignorant of the existence of the manuscript, but remained unaware that much of its contents was already in print.

Beyond indicating that the manuscripts of 1712 and 1716 had a single owner early in the nineteenth century, the *Panoplist* is of no assistance. The documents are introduced with the unproductive comment that "an obliging friend has favored us with the

Diary kept by Cotton Mather . . ." (XII, 362). Nor have I been able to discover the identity of the "friend" by checking the records of the Congregational Library for information concerning acquisition of the companion manuscript of 1716. Thus, in spite of a number of possible leads, the history of ownership remains to be established. The matter of considerably more importance, however, is that, as a kind of supplement to Ford, the diary be made available to scholars in a reliable modern edition.

The *Panoplist* is difficult to come by. Moreover, its version of the diary does not represent a reliable edition. Its compilers felt perfectly free to alter and to delete as they saw fit, sometimes seriously changing meaning in the process. On occasion, though rarely, they resort to untruth in the desire to make Mather's position jibe with their own more ecumenical views. Specifically, Mather's frequent, contemptuous references to the superstitions or iniquities of the Church of England (to which he ordinarily refers as the "Ch. of E.") The *Panoplist* does not tone down: it either omits entirely the offending entry (4.G.D., p. 41), sentence (1.G.D., p. 87), or phrase (1.G.D., p. 91), or maintains untruthfully that (as in 5.G.D., p. 76) "the author here left the manuscript imperfect." Consequently, the *Panoplist* even when available cannot be relied on.

In spite of its editorial willingness to alter both style and content, the *Panoplist* presents a reasonably accurate text for the approximately seventy per cent of the manuscript which it prints. In general, the changes in phraseology result either in making more concise what in the original exemplifies Mather's swelling verbosity or in avoiding archaic structures (or diction) in the interest of nineteenth-century "grammatical" propriety. The result is to heighten the formality of an already somewhat stiff personal document. More serious are those alterations which are obviously intended to present Mather in a light different from that cast by his own words. Most often these changes amount to the simple omission of passages reflecting either of two Mather characteristics: intolerance or personal vanity. Aside from their tendency to mislead, such prudent omissions intensify what is already a marked and, one might add, rather frustrating feature of the typical Mather diary—abstraction and vagueness. And, finally, suppression of material reflective of Mather's personality simultaneously suppresses that which, above all, a Mather diary is best prepared to offer—one of its basic sources of interest.

One matter yet remains to complete the history of publication, or more exactly, of near publication. In the library of the Massachusetts Historical Society is an annotated edition of the diary of 1712 consisting partly of typescript "based on photostats of the original" and partly of snippets cut from the *Panoplist* with appropriate corrections inked in. The document is identified as a "Typescript . . . annotated by Allyn B. Forbes . . . prepared for publication in Volume 64 [Oct. 1930—June 1932] of *Proceedings,* but not used." Mr. Forbes adds that "the editorial work . . . has been made to conform to that" of the Ford edition of 1911–12. Though I have not sought a similar conformity and have, for instance, annotated more fully than Mr. Forbes, I have occasionally found his notes extremely helpful and have not hesitated, with proper acknowledgment, to use them.

II

When, after noting that the "diary of 1712 is not preserved," Professor Wendell adds that he finds in Samuel Sewall's diary for that year "nothing especial about [Mather], except that he went to Commencement," [3] he indirectly defines one of the basic differences between Mather's diary and Sewall's. For it is precisely the particular fact that abounds in Sewall for which one turns in vain to Mather. And here is Mr. Wertenbaker's justification for asserting that "Mather's *Diary* [is] less important than Sewall's as a historical document." [4] The charge cannot be denied. The minister's diary often makes dull reading, but for reasons opposite to

[3] *Ibid.*
[4] Thomas Jefferson Wertenbaker, *The Puritan Oligarchy* (New York, 1947), p. 93.

those which often make the Judge's equally dull. Whereas the
latter bogs down by its very mass of ungeneralized particulars, some
of which the historian can find useful, the former moves serenely
among the upper reaches of "historically" uninformative abstraction—its author apparently governed by disdain for the specific,
concrete, and detailed.

Time and again he seems perversely determined not to specify
by name the objects of his notice. Thus the diary contains innumerable references to unidentified individuals in both their
public and their private capacities and to vaguely suggested con-
temporary affairs of both local and international concern. Though
usually Mather gives enough information to make identification
possible, he does not always do so; and in any event, one can
scarcely avoid annoyance with a man who insists on referring to
people as, for instance, "that boisterous fellow on the Indian Commission," "a woman of much importance and evil influence in the
world," "my old classmate's uncle," "my kinsman in the Indian
service," or "my wife's brother's eldest nephew." Still more exas-
perating are the references to unspecified "calamities," "judgments," "sins," "catastrophes," "burglaries," and other "enormities." In short, though there is much to learn in a Mather diary,
and though there is an entry for every day of the year, one must
turn to Sewall to discover such mundane facts as Mather's attendance at Harvard commencement.

All years were of the most dreadful import to Mather's strained
sensibilities, 1712 being no exception. One constantly feels his
awareness that events of the most stupendous significance to what
alone is to him of real importance—Christ's kingdom—are presently taking place. But all too often he only hints at the exact
nature of these happenings. On the level of world affairs, the
momentous concerns which weigh so heavily on him this year have
largely to do with the approaching Peace of Utrecht. This, as it
relates to the "Protestant interest here and abroad," and other
matters such as the encroachments of Anglicanism in Scotland and
—Lord help us!—in New England itself, bulk large in the omi-

nous though ill-defined historical background. So too with the local misunderstandings and squabbles of which New England's church and political history has been so prolific. But for Mather there is no real distinction between the merely local and the international.

In his mind all issues, whether seemingly large or small, are in a sense equalized, for all are involved in the wars of the Lord—working either in the interests of God and Cotton Mather or in those of Satan, which is another way of saying that to Cotton Mather all issues, no matter how remote they appear, are personal issues. So what we get in a Mather diary is not exactly history, but a reflection of the various ways in which historical events, local and international, impinge upon the neurotic but brilliant mind of Cotton Mather, perhaps the least loved and at the same time most interesting of New England's early personalities.

Certain occurrences within his own Church, the Second or Old North, to which he and his father Increase ministered jointly, offer a case in point. He responds with calm satisfaction to news that more seats are needed, a clear sign that there is an increase among those "Who Prize the Ministry here," that his own ministry in particular is prospering. But all too soon we encounter references to "murmurings" among an obstreperous flock, disobedience, lack of respect and regard for his and his father's labors. Veiled rumblings of discontent and faction are sensed in the background, and then we learn that there is talk "of our Church Swarming into a New Meeting-house." Now this is a cat of an entirely different species. Yet according to his own account, Mather behaves admirably throughout the entire difficult business, controls his temper perhaps better than during any other trying circumstance of his lifetime.

Before the establishment of the New North Church in 1713, however, his flock has become a "proud Crew, that must have Pews for their despicable Families . . . [a] boisterous, ambitious, ill-bred Company . . . who [neither] consult [nor] desire the Prosperity of . . . a Church . . . ripe for something little short of a miserable Dissolution." [5] But as always supernatural causes are at work. At one time "Satan seems to have . . . a Commission to sift the Church, and shake it wonderfully, and bring it into very diminutive Circumstances" (*Diary*, II, 195). At other times God seems to be directly responsible, and we find the harassed minister considering the possibility that the whole affair is a divine chastisement for some unremembered, but nevertheless to be repented, sin of his own committing. "I judge and loathe myself before the Lord, for all my Miscarriages, by which I may have provoked Him, to take away a Considerable part of my Flock from me" (*Diary*, II, 183). The true source of Mather's personal concern is here made manifest. Whatever the cause, whether the Divine "Energies" or the Satanic, the object of their attention has been Cotton Mather, in one sense very much alone in his egocentric universe. "I made a Sacrifice of the Flock, and of all my Opportunities to do Good in the World, unto the Great God; with a most consenting Resignation, and became willing to be a Preacher, unto a very small Auditory, and to be reduced unto very diminutive Circumstances, and to encounter any Humiliations and Annihilations, that He shall please to order for me" (*Diary*, II, 184).

Although the doleful and the ominously prophetic predominate, circumstances occasionally work in the interests of Cotton Mather. When he needs a subject for a coming sermon, an angel appears to him in a dream and suggests an admirable topic. In another instance, seriously at a loss for something to publish and disperse "among the People of God," but never doubting that the Lord "will Provide work" for him, he rejoices when his faith is justified. Clearly for the express purpose of providing His earthly agent with suitable subject matter, "The Holy God" publicly exposes "A Number of Wicked Young Men in the Town [who] have made themselves a Band of Robbers [and committed] horrid Burglaries." Mather's gratitude for this heavenly kindness is immeasurable. "Oh! What shall [I] render to my Glorious Lord! Oh! how shall I

[5] Worthington Chauncey Ford, *The Diary of Cotton Mather* (Boston, 1911–12), II, 194–95 (hereinafter referred to as *Diary*).

Love Him, and Praise Him, and Serve Him. He deals marvellously with me, He will go on, after an astonishing Manner, to make use of me, in Service for Him" (p. 49).[6]

But somewhat earlier Mather had let fall in a sermon words of a "Predictory Strain," to the effect that he "Lived in a daily and trembling Expectation" that God would "Speedily take Some of our young Men, and make them dreadful Examples of His Wrath, and hang them up in Chains for all the Congregation of our Israel to tremble at" (p. 48). And other of his prophetic utterances have been fulfilled. He remarks with satisfaction that it has become a matter of "Common observation" that when he warns his auditors that some of them may never again be so fortunate as to hear another sermon, the subsequent week "is then Signalized with Some very observable Mortality." Oblivious of the fact that the death of a fellow human being is no more suitable a cause for ministerial exultation than is the unexpected discovery that juvenile delinquency is rampant in the town of one's spiritual ministrations, Mather glories in these further evidences of his election, in such happy events "whereby," as he almost too candidly puts it, "a Great Authority is Conciliated unto my Ministry." Satisfied that his communications with the will of God are still intact, he considers publicly declaring his "Strong Impression" that "It will not be Long before we see [other of Boston's young people] . . . in very woeful Circumstances," a thought he finds so encouraging as to demand repetition. The discussion of this incipient prophecy concludes with a remark the piety of which is balanced only by its disturbing ambiguity: "It may be, the Lord, will bless this Declaration to do some good among them" (p. 59).

One is tempted to insert here some scathing comment relevant to Mather's corruption for egocentric ends, of the providential interpretation of history: the noble idea that all history is nothing less than the dramatic unfolding in time of the Divine will. But to do so would be unfair to Mather. It is, then, necessary to resist

[6] Absence of a volume number indicates that reference is to the present diary of 1712, and not to Ford's edition of the *Diary*.

the temptation and parenthetically to enter certain qualifying remarks at this point. That the idea seems degraded here and that Mather looks meanest when meditating particular providences in largely personal terms, something both he and his father were prone to do, belie the fact that his philosophy always remains fully inclusive of the larger view. Although he compiled the *Magnalia Christi Americana* some fourteen years earlier, in 1712 he still maintains the complex of enthusiasm, belief, feeling, and idea that had enabled him to create in his ecclesiastical history what is at once the most interesting, the fullest, and the most dramatic rendering in prose of that theory of the historical process.

That he accepts simultaneously the "scientific" principle of the regularity of natural law and the "superstitious" principle of divine intervention identifies something of the paradoxical nature of Mather's mind. To be at once a superstitious bigot, a participating member of the Royal Society, an intellectual throwback in always forward-looking Boston, and the "First Significant Figure in American Medicine" [7] is, after all, something of an accomplishment. We must not forget that it is precisely in his diaries that Mather looks least attractive. Nor should we forget that, as a result of the almost total change in world view since his time, Mather looks least attractive of all from the perspective of that newer complex of chilling thought and disillusion which Joseph Wood Krutch calls "the modern temper." This amounts to saying that to give Mather his due requires a particularly strenuous, perhaps impossible, effort of historical adjustment. Keeping these qualifications in mind we may once again turn our attention to the diary.

As Mather's references to sermons and publications indicate, events end for him neither with their happening nor with their personal impact; they can and should be put to further use as edification for making others better or, to use his favorite periphrasis, of doing them good. To an extraordinary degree Mather believes

[7] Otho T. Beall, Jr., and Richard H. Shryock, "Cotton Mather: First Significant Figure in American Medicine," American Antiquarian Society, *Proceedings*, n.s., LXIII (1953), 37–274.

in the efficacy of the spoken and written word as a means of moral reform. As a result, he is constantly on the lookout for materials to work up in sermon or lecture, which in turn, whenever possible, he positively delights in seeing appear in print. An election, an "observable" death, the installation of a minister, the loss of a ship at sea—each calls for the preparation of a sermon. Indirectly then, the sermons themselves, though clearly not recordings of history in the usual sense, constitute a kind of running commentary on it. To the genesis of these and other of his writings Mather devotes considerable space in the diary, and it is largely in this oblique fashion that historical events manage to get in at all. When they do, furthermore, the emphasis is less on the events for their own sake than on the "suitable admonitions of Piety" Mather can draw from them, on the use to which he can put them in his never-ceasing efforts to do good.

In stressing the good he hopes to accomplish Mather reverses customary diary procedure by placing the burden on the future instead of the past. This characteristic suggests a peculiarity which the diary of 1712 shares with those of 1711 and of all subsequent years. A striking if not very appealing feature of these documents consists in the recording for each day a numbered "G.D." or "Good Devised," an intention to perform some benevolent action in accordance with a formula which ascribes to each day of the week a particular object for such attentions. According to this formula, entries marked "1.G.D." (for Sunday) are to concern his "FLOCK," "2.G.D." (Monday) his "FAMILY," while alternate Tuesdays ("3.G.D.") are to concern "RELATIVES ABROAD" and *"personal Enemies."* On Wednesday ("4.G.D.") he plans to consider what good he can do *"in the Country,* or among other People"; on Thursday ("5.G.D.") what *"Service"* he can render *"the* SOCIETIES"; and on Friday ("6.G.D.") what *"Objects of Compassion"* he can assist. On Saturday ("7.G.D.") he will devote himself to the all-important question: *"What remains to be done for the Kingdom of God in* MY OWN HEART AND LIFE?" (*Diary,* II, 24–28). Excepting those Tuesdays set aside for consideration of *"per-*

sonal Enemies" which instead, much to our sorrow, almost invariably concern his relatives either "ABROAD" or at home, Mather adheres rather closely to this announced plan for ordering his thoughts and structuring what he likes to call his "reserved Memorials."

As a result, the later diaries consist of daily, numbered, but undated notes of Mather's pious intentions interspersed with occasional, dated entries descriptive of what he actually has done. Though he frequently permits one and sometimes as many as three weeks to pass without a date, it can always be established for a given passage by counting forward from the last dated entry. By its very nature the system provides a kind of index in reverse, at least for those categories of entry which it embraces. Since Mather does not invariably adhere to it, however, and since certain categories overlap, the system has perhaps more of a curiosity value than anything else. It is not for this reason less attractive to Cotton Mather, whose appetite for the unusual is voracious.

Nothing, in fact, could be more characteristic of the man than this proposed and for the most part realized regimen. He seldom asks whether or not surface regularity reflects a meaningful principle of organization within; so long as a plan has the appearance of order and system, Mather approves it. He seems to feel that the good life in part consists of cramming every hour and every minute with innumerable, itemized projects; to waste a moment, to fail in redeeming the time, he considers an unforgivable sin. It never seems to occur to him that pursuing a given routine over and over, day after day, year after year, might result in a "piety" more mechanical and formal than spiritually meaningful. His perfect sincerity cannot be doubted. Somehow, just to get a thing in writing seems to be for him a means of giving life meaning and purpose, and he repeatedly urges his children to inscribe in their "Blank Books" whatever they have done, read, heard of, or plan to do that might lead to their salvation or provide evidence of it. But the big thing after all is always to be doing something, and a written plan is a means of always having something to do, though at times one suspects that the writing itself—sometimes the mere copying from one "Memorial" to another—provides at least as much satisfaction as the doing, which at its worst becomes an acting out, a mere posturing.

Yet for Mather the recording of a deed, whether proposed or already accomplished, is not an ending end. A firm believer in the values of the moral injunction, the "admonition of Piety," Mather nevertheless endorses with all his heart the doctrine that "Good *Patterns* do a great deal more *Good* in this World than Good *Precepts*." [8] And his expressed purpose for writing the diary is at least twofold: "These papers being written for the Instruction of my Children, after I am Dead, as well as for my own Reflection upon them, before I die, I would Serve every Interest of Piety in them, from my own Experience" (p. 66). Not only would he make his life worthy to be followed, he would also render it more readily imitable by committing it to writing in order that "mine," as he says, "may go and do Likewise." The didactic intention substantially differentiates a Mather diary from the habitual, largely unself-conscious jottings of a Samuel Sewall on the one hand and absolutely from such entirely personal journals as *The Secret Diary* of Virginia's William Byrd on the other. The purpose of these is private; the purpose of Mather's is at least partly public. In his, a conscious principle of selection is always operative.

Yet paradoxically, a Mather diary is not less revealing than these or others which resemble them. Somehow in spite of his stupendous learning and the complexity of his character there is about Mather's personality a curiously naive transparency. His every action reveals its motivation, which invariably comprehends a mixture simultaneously conducive to the greater glory of God, the reformation of mankind, and the magnification of Cotton Mather. The last of these is most readily and consistently apparent to the modern mind, which tends either to reject as conscious rationalization Mather's avowed intentions or, perhaps more generously, but still from a position of assumed superiority, to find in the per-

[8] *The Good Old Way* (Boston, 1706), p. 1.

sonal aggrandizement the expression of a subconscious compulsion which reveals itself, even as it achieves a kind of fruition, in his unceasing efforts to render unto God by doing good in the world.

In a very real sense Mather's diary can be considered, as can his entire conscious life, one colossal "Good Devised." He strives to live as he conceives a Christian should, and he records for his own future imitation those of his past actions which he considers worthy; he projects innumerable plans for his future behavior in order that he may continue to improve in piety. Where the pinch comes for us is that he does not leave the matter there but insists, and openly at that, on setting up his own life as an example for his children to follow that they too may "Live unto God." This purpose is, of course, closely analogous to that of the biographies which he produced in such alarming numbers. Most of the *Magnalia*'s roughly seventy lives are intended to serve as examples for imitation. With this in mind we can accept on its own terms Mather's glorification of those whose biographies he writes; but we find it difficult, almost impossible, not to see in the setting-up of his own life as a similar example the expression of a vanity that has achieved cosmic proportions. That he is vain is perfectly evident, but a good deal more is involved here than mere personal vanity.

Praise of good men is really praise of God, adumbration of His powers and virtues. For, as Samuel Mather insists prior to the purely eulogistic description of his father, "These are the *Graces* which adorned this *Man* of GOD: But GOD forbid that we should ascribe *any Thing* to him! No! *The Grace of* GOD is to be praised, that was pleased to fill him with *these and other Rational and Religious Ornaments.*" [9] In other words, look around or through the virtues and graces of the man described to the original Donor in Whom they are absolute. "In Reading of all *History*," Cotton Mather implores, "ever now and then make a convenient Pause; to think, *What can I see of the Glorious* GOD *in these Occur-*

[9] *The Departure and Character of Elijah Considered and Improved* (Boston, 1728), p. 25.

rences." [10] And he provides specific instructions on reading biographies written in accordance with Matherian formulas: "Truly, whatever was Excellent in these our *Johns,* I would pray, that the Minds of all that see it, may be raised still to think, *Our Precious Lord Jesus Christ, is greater than these Johns:* All their *Excellencies* are in Him Transcendently, Infinitely; as they were from *Him* derived. *High Thoughts* of the Lord Jesus Christ, provoked by *Reading* the Descriptions of these his *Excellent* Servants, that had in them a little of *Him,* and were no farther *Excellent* than as they had so, will make me an abundant Recompense, for all the Difficulties, and all the Temptations, with which my *Writing* is attended." [11] As the diary suggests, and as "Paterna" makes explicit,[12] Mather sought to pattern the spirit of his own life on Christ's. Just as in the case of "our *Johns,*" the plea is for the reader to consider not the virtues of the man, but what there is of Christ in the man, for only in this respect is any life truly exemplary. Therefore we must recognize that his autobiographical writings signify less the life of Cotton Mather considered as a model than the pattern to which Cotton Mather strives to make his own life conform—the pattern, as he sees it, of the true Christian.

With regard to the *Magnalia* Barrett Wendell states that "somehow, as no one else can, Cotton Mather makes you by and by feel what the Puritan ideal was: if he does not tell just what men were, he does tell just what they wanted to be, and what loyal posterity longed to believe them." [13] This remark is very right and with one important qualification can be applied to the autobiographical works which resemble the biographies in that what they depict tends to the ideal as much as the actual. But the diaries, in spite of the principle of selection, define not only what Mather wanted to be but reveal with perfect clarity precisely what he was. It is partly in the distance between these poles that the fascination lies. True

[10] *Manuductio ad Ministerium* (Boston, 1726), p. 59.

[11] *Magnalia Christi Americana* (London, 1702), III, 13.

[12] The manuscript of "Paterna," Mather's unpublished autobiography, is in the University of Virginia Library.

[13] *Cotton Mather: The Puritan Priest,* p. 161.

enough, Sewall's *Diary* reveals similar poles, but the Judge, though less comical, is at the same time less interesting for the simple reason that in his case the distance between the poles is not so great. Not that his accomplishments are greater; his sights are simply aimed lower. And for all his sense of mundane responsibility, much the same is true of Byrd, or for that matter, of Franklin. It is to be lamented that so much that appears ridiculous in Mather stems directly from that in him which is most worthy of respect.

Since there could be no better way of imitating Christ than to suffer, Mather occasionally indulges in thoughts of martyrdom. But true martyrdom requires complete acceptance and the fact remains that he is constitutionally incapable of really forgiving his enemies, although he derives considerable satisfaction from telling himself that he has done so. The obvious delight he takes in calling them names and in leaving them entirely in the hands of an angry God reveals the extent of his unforgiveness. "I . . . Carried my Dangerous, Venomous, Furious Enemies, unto the Lord. And Especially one of them, who is a more Finished Rake, and Venomous and Vicious beyond many others; and besought of the Lord, that an Horror of Conscience might fall upon him; Yea! that good may be done unto him" (p. 17). The tone is scarcely Christian. Though he is aware that pride is his besetting sin, there is much truth in the assertion that of all our early writers Cotton Mather understands himself least.

On reading such a passage as the foregoing, one tends to remember Professor Schneider's amusing comment that "whenever sinners become convinced that they are instruments in the hand of God, elected to carry out his holy will, they lose their piety and begin doing good to others."[14] But Mather has strictures against too hearty an indulgence in what he calls "that odd Action, *Laughter* . . . [which] seems to be Little Other, than a Sudden Triumph of Pride, upon our Perceiving of Others to be in Circumstances inferiour to our own; but most of all, upon a Quick Apprehension, that the Follies of Others, are such as we are not

[14] Herbert W. Schneider, *The Puritan Mind* (New York, 1930), p. 264.

ourselves Guilty of. . . . And, if in the issue, I find myself con-
fined unto a Perpetual Seriousness, where is the Damage of it?
Never do we read of our Great Saviour, that at any time *He
Laughed*" (p. 77).

The ideal is a high one—the very highest—and he is completely
sincere in his lifelong efforts to approach it and to convince himself that he has on occasion met with a measure of success. The apparent posturings are simply the necessarily finite, and hence
slightly ridiculous, efforts of a man, with perhaps more than his fair
share of human frailties, to devote his life entirely "unto God."
Nor is he alone in having devoted a lifetime to such efforts. To
the twentieth-century mind such a voluminous "record of prayers,
confessions, resolves, interior experiences, with here and there a
fact or a comment upon men and things" [15] seems fantastic and
difficult to take seriously. But here Chandler Robbins is discussing
not the diary of Cotton Mather at all, but that of his father Increase, the "Foremost American Puritan." That the description so
beautifully fits the diary of the son suggests that he, for all his
marked individuality of character, is distinctly representative of a
type: that paradoxical type of the "Puritan Priest" so ably defined
by Barrett Wendell.

Mather, who has also been called "the quintessence of Puritanism," in fact, sums up the final stage of the Puritan movement,
that stage in which, according to Alan Simpson, the "crusading
force of immense energy . . . [which characterizes the origins of
Puritanism] has everywhere subsided from an ecstasy of zeal into
standardized patterns of behavior . . . as men who had dreamed
of a holy Community . . . [find] themselves simply the adminis-
trators of a Puritan tradition." [16] What is striking in Mather is his
passionate struggle to rekindle the zeal at a time when it was already effectively dead. In this indefatigable effort lies much that

---

[15] Chandler Robbins, *A History of the Second Church, or Old North* (Boston, 1852),
p. 61.
[16] *Puritanism in Old and New England* (Chicago, 1955), p. 39.

we find at once most admirable and most pitiful in the man.

In these respects, as in every feature of his personality, Mather epitomizes what Professor Simpson calls "one of the characteristic weaknesses of the Puritan character—its want of proportion." [17] And once again we encounter paradox; for precisely in its characteristic weakness is the source of its greatest strength. For all his faults, Mather tried; no man throughout a lifetime ever tried harder. He was, of course, from the very beginning destined to failure. Yet one finally comes, I think, to agree with Wendell "that there is still good ground for believing that it was a good man they buried on Copp's Hill one February day in the year 1728." [18]

III

In this edition, Mather's spellings for the most part have been modernized, and such abbreviated forms as "o^e" for "our" and "y^e" for "the" have been spelled out. Mather's punctuation, italics, capitalization, and paragraph indentations have been retained. Marginalia have been run into the text and identified by footnotes.

Usually Mather's handwriting is neat and, under normal circumstances, easy to read. Furthermore, the apparent readiness with which he found expression for his thoughts results in a document singularly free of such blemishes as the erasures, blottings, or revisions which so often make a manuscript illegible. The most frequent difficulties result from his penchant for inserting supplementary information, or qualifying remarks, in the margins. Here too he is usually quite readable, though the script is often microscopic because of restricted space. Evidently, moreover, he sometimes transcribes from a title page or an already prepared draft. Consequently, the manuscript has almost no lacunae and only two or three passages the meaning of which is obscure. The manuscript itself is in an excellent state of preservation. As a result of

[17] *Ibid.*, p. 5.
[18] *Cotton Mather: The Puritan Priest*, p. 3.

these features, editing has required a minimum of guesswork and emendation. Where either has been necessary, I have tried to supply it with a self-explanatory, bracketed insertion.

The comparative ease of establishing a correct text has been balanced by the problem of annotation. Partly owing to their prevailing vagueness, it is a characteristic of Mather diaries that although one might justifiably annotate almost everything, there are very few instances where a note is positively required. Though making no attempt at completeness, I have annotated rather more copiously than Ford. I have done so in hope that scholars will find the notes useful and that casual readers will find in their greater specificity a welcome relief from Mather's habitual abstraction. Further justification lies in difference of magnitude. Our diary is rather brief; the Ford edition runs to better than fourteen hundred pages distributed over two volumes.

Mather's manuscript is a quarto volume with pages 19.3 cm. long and 15.4 cm. wide with some slight variation in page size. The make-up is as follows: a single leaf; 7 gatherings of 4 ll. each; a 4-leaf gathering with a (fifth) single leaf inserted after the third leaf; 2 4-leaf gatherings; 9 2-leaf gatherings; a single leaf; a 2-leaf gathering. Thus, an appropriate collational formula for the volume is: [unsigned: 1_1 $2-8^4$ 9^4 (9_3+1) $10-11^4$ $12-20^2$ 21_1 22^2]. The diary then has 63 leaves, and none of the pages are numbered (except those of gathering 18). Gathering 18 (ll. 55–56) is printed, and the 4 pages of the gathering are numbered 1–4. Except for gathering 18, the paper is laid watermarked paper all of one lot; the watermark, a coat of arms, together with the countermark, a crown with the initials "AR," is number 469 in Edward Heawood's *Watermarks Mainly of the 17th and 18th Centuries, Monumenta Chartae Papyraceae,* I (Hilversum, Holland, 1950), plate 78. The paper can be dated, then, as *ca.* 1710–11. The paper of gathering 18, which is from a different lot, is laid paper in which the spacing of the chainlines differs from that of the chainlines in the other paper. No watermark is visible in the two leaves of this gathering. The volume is unbound. The gatherings are stabbed and "oversewed" (that is, threads run from the stab-holes in front over the spine to the holes in back).[19]

To have devoted the Introduction to biographical matters would have been an act of supererogation. Professor Murdock wrote my defense some years before I had heard of the third and last of Boston's great ministerial triumvirate of Mather: "The story of Cotton Mather's life has been often told. There are many brief sketches of his career, and two full-length biographies. One of these, Barrett Wendell's *Cotton Mather,* is so excellent a study of its difficult subject as to make quite superfluous any attempt to rewrite the tale." [20] The only full-length biography of Mather to appear since Murdock made this statement is that of Ralph and Louise Boas,[21] which, though useful, by no means supersedes Wendell's earlier work. Murdock himself produced for the *Dictionary of American Biography,*[22] Vol. XII (1933), what is the finest of the "brief sketches"; and his *Selections from Cotton Mather* constitutes the best available introduction to the Puritan minister. For Mather's "place" in New England's intellectual history, the work of Perry Miller, particularly his *The New England Mind: From Colony to Province,* is indispensable.

[19] I am indebted to Mr. Kendon Stubbs of the Alderman Library for the information in this paragraph.

[20] *Selections from Cotton Mather* (New York, 1926), p. ix. The "full-length" biography referred to but not named is Abijah P. Marvin's *The Life and Times of Cotton Mather* (Boston, 1892).

[21] *Cotton Mather: Keeper of the Puritan Conscience* (New York, 1928).

[22] Future reference to the *Dictionary of American Biography* will be in the form *DAB.*

The Diary of
Cotton Mather, D.D., F.R.S.
for the Year 1712

The Lth Year of
my Life

12.d 12.m 1711 Tuesday.[1]

MY SOUL is this Day exceedingly but Very Variously affected
with the Circumstances, which I find myself called this Day to take
Notice of. This Day I finish the Forty-ninth year of my Age. Seven
times Seven years, has this unprofitable tree, been Standing in the
Field of the Lord. My God, I am astonished, I am overwhelmed,
with a Variety of Considerations. But I Set apart this Day to Prosecute them; with Fasting, and Prayers, and Praises, and Psalms, and
Alms, before the Lord.

I first, bewailed before the Lord, the Sins of my Life; and more
particularly, the Miscarriages of the Last year; most Especially, in
that though I had such cause to Look on it as Likely to be the Last
year of my Life, Yet I did not Spend it Like such an one.

The principal Miscarriages, that I discovered in the conduct of
the Year, were; First, My too Slothful and sleepy Mornings. And,
Secondly, My Remissness about the education of My Family; on
which I have not been so Intent as a Parent hastening out of the
world, and willing to Leave Excellent Children in it, should have
been.[2]

---

[1] Mather, in accordance with "legal-year" practice, considered March, not January, to be the first month of the year. "12.d 12.m" stands, then, for the twelfth of
February—his birthday and the date on which he began each year's diary.

[2] Mather's first wife, Abigail (Phillips) Mather, who died in 1702, bore him nine

3

I implored and obtained from the Enthroned JESUS, the Pardon of these, and all My Miscarriages.

I next acknowledged unto the Lord, his many Favours to me in my Life; but with much particularity those with which the year Last Expired has been beautified. My Health, in Special, and the Smiles of Heaven on my Ministry, and on my Family; and the many Services wherein the Sovereign Grace of Heaven has Employed me; and the Kindnesses I have had from Considerable Friends; and the Triumphs I have had over the malice of my Contemptible Enemies. I Saw and owned my Lovely JESUS in such things as these.

I proceeded then to Commit the Concerns of the Ensuing year; into the Hands of my Glorious Lord, and beseech Him to Smile upon me, in many enumerated Articles; but Peculiarly in this; That I may be used in doing many Singular and Excellent Things for the Advancement of His Kingdom.

I also Resigned my Life unto Him, as unto the Lord of my Life. I declared, that if He Called me to Die this year, I would with His Help, Cheerfully Submit unto it; and bless Him, in that He had allowed me to Live unto Fifty, which is a Term that not One in Fifty Comes unto. Only I requested, that the Circumstances of my Death may be such, as that the Faithfulness and Compassion of Heaven may be very Conspicuous in them; and that my Spirit may be Safe in the Hands unto which it has been so many times, and is now again deposited. But then I Presented my Supplications, that I may be Spared this year also.

Finally. I thought I would Somewhat Rectify my Method of Living for the Ensuing year, by assigning particular works unto particular Times, with so much Resolution, that nothing but what

---

children. Of these, only four were still alive in 1712: Katharine, about twenty-two; Abigail, about eighteen; Hannah, fifteen; and Increase, or "Cressy," thirteen. Filling out the family of the fifty-year-old minister were Elizabeth, eight; Samuel, six; and Jerusha, one; all were born to him by his present wife, Elizabeth (Clark-Hubbard) Mather. Of these seven children living in 1712, and out of a total of fifteen born to him during his lifetime, but two, Samuel and Hannah, survived their father's death in 1728.

is Extraordinary, (No Cry of the Sluggish Flesh) may Supersede those works at those Times.

As the Year Proceeds, I may take a more Particular Notice, of some of those Particular works. And the Purposes of this Day, will more particularly discover themselves, as they Come into operation.

Good Devised. 3.G.D. My Kinsman at *Saybrook,*[3] I would animate him, to consider himself as being Stationed in the Center of *Connecticut,* and so by degrees to Contrive how he may Extend Influences of Piety through all that Colony. And as One Essay that way, I would now send him as many Little Books of, *Seasonable Thoughts on Mortality,*[4] accommodated unto the present State of that afflicted people, as there are Towns in the Colony, and request him to send one into Each of the Towns, with, *Given to be Lent,* written upon it.

4.G.D. I have now in View, a prospect of doing a very great Service for the Christianized Indians, by producing a better Cohabitation among them. I would pursue it, and especially address and engage the Governor,[5] to fall in with the Intention.

5.G.D. In the Ruins of Two Dissolved Societies,[6] I may find Materials, to Compose One, that may do Excellent Services for the

---

[3] Rev. Azariah Mather (1685–1737), minister at Saybrook, son of the Rev. Samuel Mather of Windsor and Hannah (Treat) Mather, receives occasional mention elsewhere in his cousin's diaries.

[4] Mather's sermon *"occasioned by the raging of a Mortal Sickness in the Colony of Connecticut, and the many Deaths of our Brethren there" (Diary,* II, 156), was delivered at "BOSTON-Lecture" on January 24, 1711/12, and printed by Timothy Green in the following month.

[5] Joseph Dudley. For more on the "Cohabitation" of the Christianized Indians, see the entry for July 22 (p. 53).

[6] "Cotton [Mather] cut through the thickening layers of insulation that threatened to seal him off from the world he longed to make a great impact upon, by the little clubs he initiated which he called Reforming Societies. These private organizations, depending on neither church nor state, furthered such projects as better manners, charity, and good works in general—all to mobilize public opinion on the side of piety, reestablish a bygone unity, and provide for the maximum longevity of Puritanism in the teeth of modern times." (Cyclone Covey, *The American Pilgrimage* [Stillwater, Oklahoma, 1960], p. 63.) Professor Covey paraphrases from Perry Miller,

Kingdom of God in the Neighbourhood. I would endeavour it.

6.G.D. There is a Poor Aged, Pious, Maid, above Ninety years of Age, whose condition on some accounts Calls for my Compassion; and with it, I must Visit her.

7.G.D. That I may the more Effectually Remember my many Projections, to improve in Piety, I would hasten to Cull the Chief of them, out of my Memorials, and insert them in my *Paterna;* [7] that I may often peruse them, and by the perusal thereof imprint them on my memory.

$$\frac{\text{16.d}}{\text{17.d}} \text{ 12.m Saturday night.}$$

In a *Vigil,* I made a Visit unto Heaven, and an Address unto my Glorious Lord there Sitting on a Throne of Grace. I implored and obtained of Him, the pardon of my sins. And I besought this Favour of Him, that I might be employed by Him, to make His Glories more considered in the world, than ever they have yet been since the World began; and that therefore He would Smile upon my Ministry, and especially upon Some Essays of it, relating to this Intention, which I have now before me. I also besought Him, that I might have Good News Ere Long from *England,* and some Further Encouragements to my Services. But then I complained unto Him, of the Malice which a Number of Enemies in this place bear unto me. I praised Him, for the Strange Deliverance from the Effects of that Malice, which I had received. I prayed Him, to take me still under His protection, and work wonderfully for me. Finally, I begged, the continuance of my Life, at those Hands which have the Keys of Hades in them. And I Committed my children into those Gracious and Fatherly Hands,

---

The New England Mind From Colony to Province (Cambridge, 1953), to which the reader is referred for a full discussion of these matters. See in particular the chapter entitled "Do-Good," pp. 395–416.

[7] In this most strange "autobiography" Mather plays the curious game of attempting to conceal his identity from the reader. See also n. 28.

that when they shall be made Orphans, they may be well provided for.

Having Spread these and other Desires before the Lord, until the Sun had made a Progress in his Return unto us, from the meridian of the other Hemisphere, I applied myself to sing some Suitable Things. It surprised me, that my Psalmbook opened at that Passage; Psal-CXIX. 148.

> *Mine Eyes did timeously Prevent*
> *the Watches of the Night;*
> *That in thy Word with Careful Mind*
> *then Meditate I might.*

Without my turning over another Leaf, Several other Passages in Psal. CXIX. And in CXX. CXXI. CXXIV. were Sufficient for me. So *God my Maker,* did without a Metaphor, *give me Songs in the Night.*

1.**G.D.** A multitude of *Dreams* there are, which deceive a multitude of *Souls* in my Flock. I would faithfully warn them, and wake them, with a Discourse on that Subject.

2.**G.D.** My Consort, from whose hand I most choose it, Obliges me with bringing me my short Breakfast herself, and Sitting with me, while I am Drinking of it. I will Endeavour, that whenever She so comes to me, and Sits with me, I will communicate some useful Thought unto her.

3.**G.D.** There are at *Stratford,* Several Persons at a distance Related unto me; I would Endeavour by the first Opportunity, to Send Certain Instruments of Piety unto them.

4.**G.D.** Having an Opportunity to do it, I would in a printed Composure, Celebrate the Goodness and Courage of the Pious Matrons, who first accompanied and Encouraged their Husbands, in the Transportation hither. I would also give a Description of the Piety shining in very many of their Daughters, who have done virtuously in all Parts of the Land. I would finally, pay a Debt unto the Memory, of that Excellent woman, Mrs.

Mary Higginson,[8] whom I am under many Obligations to treat as my Mother; and Exhibit her Piety, with an agreeable Character of it. In all this, I design to do what may be done, that there may be produced a Succession of Such women, who would be the Beauties of these Colonies.

5.**G.D.** I would not only Preach about, and against *Evil Customs,* but also move the Society,[9] to unite in drawing up a *Catalogue of such Evil Customs, as are breaking in upon us.* Which we may then Publish to the Country, with Lively addresses unto Good Men, to do what they Can, for the Speedy Stopping and Curing of them.

If they decline it, I may Endeavour to do it myself.

21.d 12.m Thursday.

This Day, I enjoyed (after previous Humiliations,) a glorious Presence of the Lord with me, in preaching the Lecture,[10] to a Vast Auditory; bearing of Testimonies against *Evil Customs* getting in among us.

6.**G.D.** A Poor, Old, Sinful Man in my Neighbourhood, is languishing under Sickness, which threatens his Life. I would make the Distressed Family a Tender of all the Reliefs my House can

---

[8] Mary Higginson, second wife of the Rev. John Higginson (1616–1708) of Salem, had died on March 9, 1709. Mather paid his tribute in the "Preface" to his *Awakening Thoughts on the Sleep of Death.* (See pp. 12–13 [Feb. 29].) This work contains the following passage: "The Reverend Servant of God, who was her Consort, once pointing to her used those words unto me, *Behold, thy Mother!* Supposing *Her* as well as *My* Surviving of him. And now, I must say, *I do remember my Faults this day;* I Confess, it has been a *Faulty Omission* in me, to let so much more than Three Years roll away, while I have neglected the Commemoration in this Public and Lasting Way, which I Owed unto such a *Mother.* But I will not reckon it now *too Late,* for me to leave upon Record, a brief *Testimony* concerning that *Excellent Woman* . . . whom I have had such leave to call *my Mother,* though *Nature* has not made me so Related unto her."

[9] The Society for the Suppression of Disorders was started by Mather in 1702.

[10] This sermon was the basis of his *Advice from the Watch Tower* which Mather "sent unto the Press" on approximately May 22, 1713.

give him. And I would use my painful Endeavours for his Conversion to God. [Ματθεν Ιονες] [11]

7.G.D. 'Tis an Advice which I have Lately with great Importunity pressed upon others, that they would Seriously and Thoroughly Examine themselves on this Point; *Is there no Evil Custom, that I am in danger to be carried away withal?* Examine, *Is there no Wrong Step, to which I am accustomed?* I would myself Exceedingly Conform to this Advice; and not only this morning Employ some Time in that Examination; but also often on The Sabbath-Evening Spend some Thoughts upon it. The Chief of my *Evil-Customs,* which I am at this Instant most sensible of, are; My Rising too Late in a Morning. My Putting off the preparations of my Sermons too Late in the week. And, my being too formal in my Family Devotions.

1.G.D. There are some Contrivances relating to New and More Seats in our Meeting-house,[12] which being well prosecuted, may be of Good Consequence for the welfare of many Souls. I would first ask the Blessing and the Conduct of the Glorious Lord, for the Peaceable Management of such an affair; and then Put it into a way of Prosecution.

2.G.D. My Son *Increase,* I will now have to sit by me, especially on the Lords-day Evenings; and Read over to me, first the *Paterna* I have written for him; [13] and Such other things as may be most Suitable to him; and make them the Arguments of my most Winning Discourses with him.

3.G.D. I have a Brother-in-Law,[14] who has, I doubt, much Sinned

[11] Matthew Jones.

[12] Before culminating in a new and separate Church organization—the New North —this matter, which punctuates like a refrain the diaries of this and the following year, was to cause both pastors of the Old North considerable anguish.

[13] This provides pretty definite proof that Mather wrote "Paterna" not for Samuel, as has been generally assumed, but for the scapegrace Increase who died at sea in 1724. Following his death the father crossed out or generalized all references sufficiently specific to identify the particular son addressed and subsequent generations have, incorrectly, taken for granted that Samuel was intended.

[14] Dr. John Clark (H.C. 1687), eldest brother of Mather's second and present wife

away the Convictions and Awakenings which have been upon him, and is now Entangled in Business, and Company, which draws him sometimes into Bad Hours, with Disguising Effects thereof upon him. I must endeavour, by Prayers, by Counsels, by Sermons, and in all the Exquisite methods of goodness, to recover this Relation.

4.**G.D.** An horrid fellow has made a Mock-Sermon,[15] full of tendency to debauch the Minds of the Young People in the Place; and Spread Copies of it. I would not only on this occasion, get the Ministers to join with me, in bearing due Testimonies against the Matchless and Flagrant Impiety that has been Committed; and using all Possible Endeavours, to expell the Poison that has been insinuated into the Souls of the people, but also Write a solemn Letter to the Blasphemer himself, that may set before him the heinous and hideous Nature of his Iniquity, and Spread Copies of my Letter, that it may go into as many hands as have had the Devilish Libel in them.

27.d 12.m Wednesday.

This Day, I attended the Duties of a Fast, with South Church, Seeking to Heaven for the Blessing of Heaven on them in providing a Succession and Assistance, for the Evangelical Ministry

---

Elizabeth (Clark-Hubbard) Mather, became "a leading politician of the 'popular party'" headed by the Cookes—no friends of Cotton Mather. He served first as Justice of the Peace in 1700 and thereafter, for many years between 1708 and 1724, as "Representative from Boston" (Sibley, III, 375). Dr. Clark was "himself of the third generation of John Clarks, all physicians, and followed by a line of four more John Clarks, equally direct, also all physicians,—covering a period of more than a century and a half, and including seven generations of the same name" (*ibid.*, p. 378). See also the entries for July 29 (p. 56) and Aug. 5 (p. 59).

[15] For further information on the "Mock-Sermon," which, according to Judge Samuel Sewall, was "full of Monstrous profaneness and obscenity" and "pronounced in the *face of Government*," see Sewall's *Diary*, 3 vols., in *Massachusetts Historical Society Collections*, 5th Series (Boston, 1878), II, 336–37, and *The Letter-Book of Samuel Sewall*, 2 vols., in *Massachusetts Historical Society Collections*, 6th Series (Boston, 1888), II, 2–3.

among them. I was helped of Heaven, in some of the Services of the Day.[16]

5.G.D. It is now the Day of the Week, for my Thoughts on that question, *Is there No other Particular Person to whom I may make a Proposal, of Doing some Good that lies more in their Way than mine?* That which I now think upon, is this: Whether the Ministers of the Town, may not accompany my, *Pastoral Desires,*[17] now Lying ready for the Press; with a Testimony of their Desires, to have the Book well entertained. And, then, if the Lord Spare my Life, I would Every week for this whole year, Send Two or Three of the Books to the Ministers in the Country, successively; with insinuations unto many of them, that they may be dispersed among their people.

28.d 12.m Thursday.

While I am Continually dispensing my poor Alms, and filling my Life with Pious Expenses; even so, that Every day in the year, may pretend unto Something thereof; the Glorious Lord, my Enthroned JESUS, is wonderfully providing for me and Mine. The Presents made unto me and my Family this Last Year, amount in value, to more than, [left blank] and besides, I do this Evening Receive a

[16] Judge Sewall, a member of the South Church, records this event as follows: "Midweek, Febr. 27. Fast at the South-church in order to call a Minister. . . . Dr. Cotton Mather prayed Excellently" (*Diary*, II, 337). On April 25 the communicating members selected the Judge's son Joseph to fill the post.

[17] See p. 33 (entry for May 10). In his anxiety that his works be published, Mather occasionally resorts to tactics at best devious. Consider in this respect the following excerpts from his letter of January 11 to Samuel Penhallow: "MY HONOURED FRIEND,— . . . . I now pray your Acceptance of another small Thing; that what, I think, entertained your Ear when you were here, may now entertain your Eye.

"My Book of, PASTORAL DESIRES . . . now waits for some Help to be given unto it. I was thinking, about a Line or two of yours unto Mr. *Archer,* to this Effect; 'That C.M. having delivered in the public . . . a Discourse of *excellent Things,* and having signified . . . his Intention to publish the Discourse . . . ; it would be a Noble thing in him . . . to enable . . . C.M. to prosecute his good Intention, by a generous Tender of three or four pounds . . . to help him in the Charge of the Impression. . . .' " (quoted from *Diary,* II, 169–70).

Legacy, which a Gentleman and his Wife, who deceased a year ago, Left unto me; His is Fifty Pound; and hers is Thirty.

By these things, my Glorious Lord Encourages me to be Rich in Good works, and more Zealous of them than ever heretofore. He Encourages me to Rely yet more hopefully and joyfully on His Fatherly and Saviourly Care to provide well for me and mine. He animates me to Study yet greater usefulness, and Labour that I may be more Serviceable than other Men, on whom there are not laid such Distinguishing obligations.

6.G.D. There is a Poor Family in my Neighbourhood; wherein the Man, who is a Godly Man, is distracted; the woman has many Children; and their Poverty and Misery must needs be considerable. I would therefore immediately Visit them and Relieve them, and also take some care that they may be provided for.

There is also a very Wicked Fellow, a Corrupter of our youth, —to be brought unto Repentance—I wrote a Large Letter to him.

29.d 12.m Friday.

Though I have kept one Public Fast this Week already, yet I would not have it Supersede a Secret one: which I am therefore this Day endeavouring; with prayers and Alms going up before the Lord. The Main Intention, which I pursued this day was to Obtain from the Gracious Lord, the Pardon of my horrible Sins, which had rendered me one of the most Loathsome and Wretched Creatures upon earth before Him.

Having Lately preached a Sermon unto a private Society of Christians, concerning the *SLEEP* of *Death,* on a Text assigned me by the Master of the Family, who had Lately buried his Pious Wife, the Society were desirous to publish the Sermon. I Considered, it would give me an opportunity to inculcate some glorious Truths of the Gospel, and also to pay a Debt unto the Memory of the Pious Women who have adorned this Country; especially unto that Excellent Saint, a mother in ISRAEL, than whom I had not a Kinder Friend in the world; Mrs. *Mary Higginson.* So I gave the Treatise unto the public, under the Title of, AWAKENING THOUGHTS ON THE SLEEP OF DEATH. *A Short Essay, on the Sleep, Which by Death all men must fall into. The* **(I.)** *Meaning of that Lively Metaphor, the Nature of the Sleep, and the Method by which we may Enter into an happy Rest, when we fall Asleep. With a Debt paid unto the memory of some that Sleep in JESUS.*[18]

1712

7.G.D. When I Pay what I owe at any time, I would make it an occasion for that Acknowledgement, *O My Glorious JESUS, How Infinitely am I Indebted unto thee, who hast paid my Debt unto the Infinite Justice of God!* And for that Supplication; *O my God, Grant me this Blessing, that I may Owe no man any thing but Love*

1.G.D. When I have Opportunity to address the Several Religious Societies in my Neighbourhood, I would with a Particular, Importunate, and Written Address move it unto them, that they will Agree, Every one of them, to Stay at home, and preserve their own Families, from the too Common Way of Misspending the *Lords-day Evening.* Piety would be much promoted in the Flock, by such an Agreement.

2.d 1.m Lords Day.

My Two Principal Errands to the Table of the Lord were,

I. To Obtain with the Pardon of my Sin, from the Enthroned JESUS, a mighty Improvement in that Principle of Grace, with which a pardon is always accompanied.

II. To Obtain a Singular Degree of Wisdom and Vigour, for

---

[18] The Roman numeral, placed in the margin by Mather, indicates that this is his first printed publication of the year.

the Spending of my Time, in Such Purposes and Actions, as will Enable me to give up my Account with Joy.

2.G.D. Resolving, with the Leave and Help of Heaven, to have the Morning-Sacrifices in my Family, Precisely at Nine of the clock, Let who will be in the way, and Let whatever Business occur; I would have my Three Children who attend the Schools in the Neighbourhood, then to Step home, and to have their part in the Sacrifices.

3.G.D. My Aged Parent begins now somewhat Sensibly to impair in Strength and Health, and feel the Decays of Age.[19] I would keep therefore more close than ever to him; and study Every thing that may render his Age Comfortable, and preserve it Honourable.

4.G.D. A wretched crew pretending to be for the Ch. of E. but intending to disturb and distract the Church of Christ, at *Newbury;* [20] besides other good services, whereto I would be Excited

---

[19] Increase Mather (H.C. 1656), senior pastor of the Second Church, became seventy-three in June 1712.

[20] A fully documented account of the squabble from which the Anglican church at Newbury took its origin is given in Joshua Coffin, *A Sketch of the History of Newbury, Newburyport, and West Newbury* (Boston, 1845), pp. 175–85.

A horrified Samuel Sewall records (*Diary*, II, 838): "Feb. 27. Joseph Bailey of Newbury . . . Presented a Petition to the Governor, signed by . . . twenty-two in all, declaring that they were of the pure Episcopal Church of England, would no longer persist with their mistaken dissenting Brethren in the Separation; had sent to their Diocesan, the Bishop of London, for a Minister, and desired Protection," protection, which it might be added, the Anglican Governor Dudley was only too happy to extend.

There seems to be good reason for accepting Sewall's (and Mather's) instantaneous assumption that the action was more the result of financial than pious considerations. To "the petitioners'" request that they no longer be "obliged to contribute to the support of the dissenting teachers" Governor Dudley gave his gracious support; the indignant commentary of the Rev. Benjamin Colman, himself no stickler for the ways of "primitive congregationalism," suggests how small a part dogma and ritual played in the decision to return to the Church of England.

"Many of them," asserts Colman, "utterly ignorant of the church they declare for [are] not offended in the least with the form of worship or discipline, which they turn from . . . being till now among us the most narrow and rigid dissenters, who would before this have disowned me in particular for the use of the Lord's prayer,

on this occasion, I would immediately send unto that place, a Number of Books, which may Enlighten the people in the principles and practices, their Ignorance whereof Exposes them to much Temptation.

5.**G.D.** I would not only animate the Religious Societies in the Town where I Live; but, inasmuch as I understand, a Letter of Mine, may Revive some that are Dead in a Neighbour-Town, I would write such a Letter accordingly.

6.**G.D.** There are Ministers in some very small places, who Encounter with Low and Mean Circumstances, and some of them, if not supported from abroad, can hardly continue in Stations, where the Interests of Religion call for them. I would Relieve such myself; and obtain Relief also from others for them: Among these, I now particularly think on, *Wilson* at *Swansea.*[21]

7.**G.D.** The Resolution of More Early Rising in the morning must be Quickened and Strengthened in me, by my Considering Effectually, first, How desirable Works I may dispatch in my Morning Hours; which I may with Comfort then Look back upon; Secondly, How near probably my Time is to its period, so that I must use a more than ordinary Dispatch, or else Leave many desirable works unfinished.

1.**G.D.** One of the Greatest, and most needful Services that I can do for my Poor Flock, is with all Possible Expressiveness and Solemnity, to Set before them the Suspicious Tokens of Hypocrisy, the Marks of the Tares in the Field of the Lord: For indeed, I am afraid, I am afraid, there are too many such among them.

---

reading the scriptures and a freer admission to the Lord's table, than has been generally practised in these churches" (quoted from Coffin, p. 183). See also Sewall's *Letter-Book,* I, 416–19, and John James Currier, *History of Newbury, Mass., 1635–1902* (Boston, 1902), p. 228.

[21] Mr. Shipton (Sibley, V, 301) notes that the Rev. John Wilson (H.C. 1705), "great-grandson of the first minister of Boston . . . was preaching [in 1712] to a group of Puritans who were then trying to persuade the General Court to set them off from the Baptists of Swansea as the separate town of Barrington (now in Rhode Island). Before the new town could be set up or the church gathered, however, Mr. Wilson died . . . on November 23, 1713" at the age of twenty-seven.

This therefore I will, with the Assistance of Heaven, Endeavour to do.

2.**G.D.** Let the Evening-Sacrifices in my Family, be attended with a Revival of the Catechetical Exercises, and Let there be Still One Question in the Catechism Spoken to; and this in the most Explicatory, the most Applicatory, the most Edifying manner that can be.

3.**G.D.** My Brother-in-Law,[22] who once Enjoyed my Sister *Jerusha,* is newly married again, to a Virtuous and ingenious young Gentlewoman, and lives in my nearest Neighbourhood. I would Endeavour Such a Carriage towards both him and her, as may have a Tendency to improve them, not only in Piety, but also in Usefulness, and Likewise do my best, that they may prove great Blessings to one another.

4.**G.D.** I am thinking, Whether it might not have a desirable Tendency, to do much Good among the Scholars at the College, and among those to whom they may be employed afterwards to do Good, if certain preachers of the Churches in the Neighbourhood, should be desired and obtained, in their Courses now and then to Preach at *Cambridge.* I would propose this to the Consideration of some, who may be most able Effectually to prosecute it.

5.**G.D.** I would not Let One Day more Pass me, without having some Considerate Persons with me, to Project the Methods, and Propose the Subjects, for another Society, to Prosecute the Intention, to Do Good in the Neighbourhood.

13.d 1.m Thursday.

This Day was a General Fast, through the Province; The Lord Carried me through the Duties of it, with Precious Assistances of Heaven.

---

[22] Mather, whose sister Jerusha had died in childbirth two years before, always spoke of Peter Oliver, her husband, with marked affection. Within two months of his second marriage, Oliver himself was dead. See p. 30 (April 27).

6.G.D. There is an Aged Handmaid of the Lord, who was my Mother's Maid at the Time of my Nativity.[23] I understand, she meets with some wants and Straits. I am therefore to dispense Reliefs unto her.

7.G.D. I have not been altogether without Care to have the *Winter* accommodated with peculiar, and adapted Strokes of Piety. But the Other Three Seasons of the year, ought to have the Like Accommodation.

We are now Entering the *Spring*. And there are Certain agreeable Supplications,[24] which I would at this time of the year much insist upon.

$$\frac{15d}{16d}$$ 1.m Saturday night.

I applied myself this Night unto the Exercises of a *Vigil;* and I had my Spirit gloriously Enlightened, revived, and Comforted from above.

One Intention of my Supplications from the Dust, where I Lay Prostrate before the Lord, was, to obtain, after the Pardon of my Sins, and a fresh Assurance of it; a Mighty Presence of the Lord with me, in my Exhortations to the young people of the Town, tomorrow, and especially in my Approaching Lecture. In this Vigil, I also Carried my Dangerous, Venomous, Furious Enemies, unto the Lord. And Especially one of them, who is a more Finished Rake, and Venomous and Vicious beyond many others; and besought of the Lord, that an Horror of Conscience might fall upon him; Yea! that good may be done unto him.

[23] A Mrs. Gale.

[24] The reference is to Mather's *Winter Piety.* Concerning this work Holmes remarks (III, 1224), "The *Diary* (II, 148) under date January 2, 1711–12, mentions this work as being published 'This Week.' Perhaps more pointed observations, in Mather's characteristic style, than the sermon contains, are made upon the winter season in the *Diary* itself a few days after this, on January 19 (II, 152–53)." The so-called *"Supplicationes Hyemalis,"* contained in the passage referred to by Holmes, should be compared with the various seasonal *"Desideria"* on pp. 124–25 of the present volume. See also pp. 41–42 (June 14).

I also Renewed my Petition for the Poor Jew, for whom I have been heretofore so much Concerned.[25]

1.**G.D.** It will be a very Comprehensive Service to the Flock, if a *Free Grammar-School,* may be obtained and Erected and Supported, in the Neighbourhood. It will not only befriend the great Interest of Education, but also give me particularly precious opportunities to do good unto very many in Visiting, and in Directing of the School. I would therefore promote this matter, not only by preparing a *Memorial* for this purpose to be Laid before the Town, but also in all the other methods of prosecution.

2.**G.D.** When I am sitting with my Family, and going to utter, the Songs which my Maker has given me for the Night, the Last thing to do, before I and they retire to Rest, must be to ask of the Capable Children, these Three Questions.

> Q.1. *Have you not neglected the Religion of the Closet today?*
> Q.2. *Have you used your Pen for any Good Purpose today?*
> Q.3. *Have you done so much Good, that it may not be said, you have wholly Lost your Time today?*

3.**G.D.** I have an Aged Father-in-Law, who is Relapsed into dangerous Illness, and is probably hastening out the World. I must Visit him, and give my Kindest and Wisest Assistances unto him, to prepare him for the Kingdom of God, and carry him Comfortably through the Valley of the Shadow of Death.[26]

4.**G.D.** I foresee a precious Opportunity in my approaching Lecture, when there will be much Expectation, of what I may Speak unto the Young People of the Place, and the Gen: Assembly may be also Sitting, to give directions, and bear Testimonies, for the Interest of Piety, especially in the Rising Generation. I Will Earnestly ask the Help of Heaven and Endeavour it.

[25] See Lee M. Friedman, "Cotton Mather and the Jews," *Publications of the American Jewish Historical Society,* No. 26 (1918), pp. 201–10.

[26] Though the diaries abound with plans to prepare him for death, Col. John Phillips of Charlestown, father of Mather's first wife Abigail, managed to survive until 1726, only two years before Mather's own demise.

19.d 1.m Wednesday.

Being tomorrow, in my Lecture, to dispense Necessary and Seasonable Admonitions of Piety, I undertake a Service wherein I shall
greatly need a special Presence of the Lord, I Set myself this Day
to humble and abase myself before Him, and with Fasting and
Prayers and Alms to ask that He would graciously Assist me.

I made it an Opportunity to Judge myself before the Lord, for
all my Deficiencies in my Testimonies for Him, and all my Im-
purities and Iniquities, which have rendered me most unworthy
to be Employed in any Testimonies. From Him in my Sacrificed
and now Exalted and Enthroned Jesus, I obtained some Assurance of my Pardon.

I considered and acknowledged myself, as *Nothing;* Yea, a Vile
Thing, worse than Nothing. I wondered, at the Sovereign Grace,
that would please to use me, in the Doing of any Thing. But I
foresaw, the Sovereign Lord, would not Reject me. However, I felt
my Mind Languishing under grievous Dejections, and Discouragements, about what I have now before me.

But, inasmuch as my Design tomorrow, is, To Address and
Engage the Children of the Place, for a *Walk in Truth,* I took
this Opportunity, to make my Cries to Heaven, with a Peculiar
Importunity, for the Conversion of my own Children; that my
own Children may have the grace to take a Religious Walk, and
Keep forever in it.

5.G.D. There are some Wretched Houses in my Neighbourhood,
Horrid Nests of Serpents, and Snares for the foolish ones that
are abhorred of the Lord. I must propose them to our Societies,
and Project Methods for the Reforming of them.

20.d 1.m Thursday.

My Poor Prayers are more than answered, in the Use which the
Glorious Lord has this Day made of me. He has given me another

Opportunity to Serve Him in a Very Vast Assembly, and mightily assisted me in my Services and my Testimonies; and Caused the Things that I have Spoken, to take a deep Impression on the Minds of Multitudes.

I gave the Sermon immediately to those who Publish it; Entitled, THE WAYS AND JOYS OF EARLY PIETY. *One Essay more, to* **(II.)** *Describe and Commend, a Walk in the Truth of our Great Saviour, unto the Children of His People. With a Testimony against some Errors which many of our Children Run into. At a Time which Very much Calls for it, and in the Audience of the General-Assembly of the Massachusetts-province.*

6.G.D. There is a Very Poor, Lame, and Miserable Widow in the Neighbourhood, that Calls for my peculiar Compassions and Assistances. [Κουρτνιε] [27]

7.G.D. I Perceive I must, in my *Paterna,* make a Recollection, of my Principal Projections and Intentions to carry on my Christian *Asceticks,* that so I may frequently have Recourse unto it, and not Lose the Remembrance and Influence, and Performance, of any of my Proposals and Resolutions.[28]

1.G.D. Some Scores of Souls, Who Prize the Ministry here and Choose to sit always under it, might be Accommodated in our Meeting-house, more than there are, if there were Prudent Methods taken for it. I desire, in the first place, Earnestly to sollicit Heaven On this Occasion; that all Disturbances about it may be over-ruled; And then concert and pursue the methods, with those that are concerned.

2.G.D. Some of my Children, Two of them, have *Scorbutic* Maladies and Languishments upon them; a Third of them is troubled with Bleeding at the Nose. I would Immediately apply

[27] Kourtnie or Courtney.

[28] In the guise of anonymous autobiography, "Paterna" was ultimately to become as much a manual of devotion as a spiritual history. The bulk of its contents, moreover, as this entry suggests, are simply transcribed from the diaries with little or no change. That "Paterna" contains almost nothing not already available to his "enemies" in other manuscripts makes all the more curious Mather's efforts to conceal his identity.

myself to their Cure; But at the Same time, I would improve
their Circumstances, to awaken their preparations for Death;
and I would Mind them of the Analogous Distempers in their
Souls of which they must pray to their great Saviour, that they
may be cured.

3.**G.D.** Can I do nothing for my Widow-Sister *Biles*, that she
may be Comfortably Provided for? I would pursue this Design.
And I would also do some fresh Kindnesses, for that Orphan.[29]

4.**G.D.** It Seems a thing of great Consequence to the Safety and
Welfare of our Churches, and the preservation of Religion in
these Colonies, that there should be a Stop given unto the Design of promoting Missionaries to be sent forth by the *Society
for propagating Religion in foreign Parts,* and Supported by
them, to disturb Religion in places where it is already in our
way practised and maintained.[30] In order to this, one of the
Best Things that can be done, is to give the public a well-
attested History of their Late Scandalous Proceedings; which
accordingly I would propose unto the Ministers in my Neighbourhood, and assist unto the best of my Ability.

5.**G.D.** There are Points of History, to be collected and preserved,
relating to the Late Conduct of our Public Affairs. I will desire
a worthy Friend of Mine, to do the Public the service of making
such a Collection.

6.**G.D.** There is a Poor Family at *Wenham,* for whom, I would
not only Procure Supplies from some wealthy Persons related
unto them, in my Neighbourhood; but also myself make Additions to them.

[29] Mather's sister Elizabeth, whose husband Josiah Byles had died in 1708. For
the "Orphan" Mather Byles (1706/07–1788), clergyman, wit, and poet, see the account by Kenneth B. Murdock, *DAB*, Vol. III.

[30] Mather refers to the Society for Propagating the Gospel in Foreign Parts which,
founded in 1701, served the Episcopal interest. One of its purposes was to assail
nonconformist churches in order to attract their members back into the Establishment. It is scarcely to be wondered at that New England Congregationalists took
offense at thus being considered the objects of missionary activity and "reformation."
See Justin Winsor, *Memorial History of Boston* (Boston, 1881), II, 213–14, and
Mather's letter of Sept. 7, 1715, to Robert Wodrow (reprinted in *Diary,* II, 326–30).

28.d 1.m Friday.

This Day, I Set apart for Prayers and Alms, with Fasting before the Lord. The Occasions and Exercises of the Day, were such as are usual with me.

But I had this Addition unto them; That my son *Increase,* is lying Sick of a Fever. I thought it necessary, to cry unto the Lord, that my own Sins, and my Son's may be Pardoned, and that for the sake of the Great Sacrifice, the Lad may have his Life Spared, and may Come out of the Sickness much a Gainer, and sensibly improved in Piety.

7.**G.D.** Formerly I Resolved, that my Attendance on the Excretory Necessities of Nature, should be still accompanied, with some Holy Thoughts of a Repenting and an Abased Soul. I will now make some Addition to that Projection of Piety. The Urinary Excretions occur often Every Day. I have seen such tragical Instances of Nephritic and Ischuriac Miseries, in others that I cannot be enough Thankful for my own Deliverance from such things. And then also, an Action that Carries Humiliation with it, how justly may it Lead me, to think with Wonderment on what my Saviour will do for me, in the Advancements of the Future State. Wherefore, when I am at any time obliged unto the Urinary Discharges, I would have one or both of these Thoughts, formed in my mind; on that mean Occasion. *My God, I bless thee for Saving me from the terrible Diseases of the Wheel broken at the Cistern.* And, *O my dear JESUS; Wilt thou Ever bring this Vile Body, to the Glories and Blessings of the Heavenly Places?*

1.**G.D.** It may be of as Good Consequence in the Discharge of my Ministry, as any thing in the world, for me to make and preach the most pungent Sermon I Can Contrive, on the Importunity, wherewith prayers and cries for a work of grace on the Soul, are to be made unto God.

30.d 1.m Lords-day.

On these Errands, I Went this Day unto the Table of the Lord.

At the Administration of the Former Element, I considered, my Blessed JESUS, as having Purchased for His People, that unspeakable Gift; a Principle of Grace, to quicken them for Living unto God; and as able and willing from His Glorious High Throne, to bestow that Gift, and a Growth and Strength of Grace upon them that Look unto Him. So I Looked unto Him, first, for the Principle itself; and Looked upon my doing so, as the Beginning of the Principle. But then I addressed Him, that I might have Exceeding Large Measures of it. I Specified more particularly, the Instances of a Well grown Grace, and of a Vast Improvement in Piety, whereof I was desirous.—I have not the Time to insert them here.

At the Administration of the Latter Element, I Singled out Especially Two Virtues of Christianity, as bought for me by the Blood of my Saviour, and now to be Expected from the Throne of His Glory. The One; the Discretion to Perform the Services whereto I am Called, Seasonably, and Acceptably and to avoid the Sufferings, to which I may by any Wrong Steps, or any Rash Words, Expose myself in that Evil Time, which is Come upon the World. The other; the Diligence, to dispatch the Duties of both my Callings with Alacrity; and bring forth Very Much of that Fruit, by which my Heavenly Father may be glorified.

2.G.D. My Sick Son *Increase* is in a way of hopeful Recovery from his Fever. Oh! that the Sickness of the Lad may be Sanctified unto him, to bring him home unto God. I must cry mightily to God for this Blessing; But I must also Discourse unto the Child, in the most Exquisite and Engaging Manner that I can upon it; and I would oblige him, as soon as he can, to Write down the Resolutions of Piety, which he takes up, on this occasion.

3.G.D. The Minister of *Watertown-Farms*, is my kinsman. I will

give him all the Assistances in his Studies that I can devise.
I will Supply his Reading, with the best things I can afford
him. I will direct the Discharge of his Ministry as well as I can.
I will communicate of my Christian *Asceticks* unto him, to
render him a Man of God.[31]

4.G.D. I foresee a Manifold Service to be done unto the Interests
of Piety, and all good Interests whatsoever, by making a Collection of the *Evil Customs,* which are used in my part of the
Country, and a Proposal of something for the *Cure* of them;
and adjoin the same unto a Discourse about *Evil Customs;* and
Publish these things, and Scatter them into all the Towns of
these Colonies. I would proceed upon this Design.

5.G.D. There are many Good Things, which I would Set forward among the Ministers of the Town, with whom I am asso-
ciated. But one among the rest is this. I have thoughts of publishing a Book of *Pastoral Desires;* Expressing the Desirable
things which a faithful Minister will wish to see among his
people. I would Engage them to accompany this Book, with
their Subscribed Approbation and Attestation; and a Recom-
mendation of it unto all the Churches in the Country. There
may be many Good Consequences of such an Action.

6.G.D. There are some Desolate and Afflicted Persons at *Charlestown,* for the Relief of whose various Necessities, I am called
to do what I can.

And a Gentlewoman at *Salem,* who is my very Valuable
Friend, hearing of the Death of her Son abroad, I will with
my Letters and Books, immediately Endeavour to assist her
Good Conduct on this Distressing Occasion.

7.G.D. If I have an Occasion to inflict a Punishment of any sort,
upon an Offender; and Very Particularly, if I must dispense a
Blow unto an Offending Servant; I would make it an occasion
for me Exceedingly to find out and Confess and Bewail before
the Lord, what Offenses to Him in my own Heart and Life,

[31] William Williams (H.C. 1705) became minister at Watertown Farms, Mass.
(later Weston) in 1709.

I can be Led hereby to think upon, and seek the pardon of them, through the Blood of the Great Sacrifice, by whose Stripes I am healed.

1.G.D. The General Assembly has made a Law, to restrain Abuses of the Lords-day Evening. It might be a Sensible and Seasonable Service unto my Flock, if on this Occasion I preach a Sermon unto them, not only about the Motives, but also about the Methods, for Spending that Evening in the Exercises of Piety. I may Excite other Ministers Likewise to do the Like.

2.G.D. The Description which I have newly given the Public, of the Virtuous and Gracious Women, who have been the Ornaments of the Country; I will oblige my Three Daughters, to transcribe it into their Blank Books, and to Study it. And I will make it the Subject of my Conference with them.

3.G.D. A Gentlewoman remotely related unto my Wife has become a Tragical Instance of Impiety and Impurity. This yields me a Sad Opportunity, to Endeavour the Repentance of that Poor woman, if I can do any thing towards it. Or, to fetch revenues of honour to God, and warning to Sinners, out of her circumstances. And to Visit and Comfort her afflicted Husband.

4.G.D. I have in my Design Several Great Works for the Kingdom of my dear Saviour. It would be no Indiscretion for me, to have my Blank Books Prepared for each of them, that so I may occasionally from time to time, Lodge in them, such materials as may occur to me in my Reading and Thinking and increase my Stock to work upon, if I may Live to proceed in the works, with a closer Application.

I would propose unto *Newbury,* an Effectual way, to prevent the Temptations which a factious crew pretending to the Ch. of E. there, may Lay before the other Inhabitants, to Leave the Pure and undefiled Religion of their Ancestors, for the sake of an unchargeable Ministry. And Endeavour to bring all the Country into the Like way of Proceeding.

5.G.D. There has been a grievous Confusion at *Medford.* There is a Prospect of Putting a Period unto it if a sum of Twenty

Pounds can be advanced, for the Satisfaction of One Obstreperous person there. I would not only bear my own Part of Contributing to it, but also stir up others; that so that poor People may have the ordinances of the Gospel Settled among them.[32]

6.G.D. There is an Aged Person, in a Necessitous Condition, and Blind, whose Necessities I would Enquire into, and have them accommodated. [Υοοςτερ] [33]

7.G.D. It is Likely to be a Dreadful Time, not only in Gr. *Britain*, but here also; a Time of sad Changes and Evils. I would apply my Mind with a more than ordinary Application unto the Thoughts of the Methods of Piety, which I am to take, that I may be accounted worthy to Escape the Evils of this Time.

1.G.D. I will mightily press upon my Hearers, the Consideration of these Two Questions; and I would Conclude my next Sermon with pressing of it.

> Q.1. *What have I yet left undone, the omission whereof would make my Death uneasy to me, if I were now to die immediately?*

> Q.2. *If I were immediately to appear before the Judgment Seat of God, what Plea have I, and what Hope, for the Blessedness of the Righteous, to be bestowed upon me?*

2.G.D. And I will with all possible Cogency oblige my children to think seriously on these two most awful Questions.

3.G.D. In the Family of my dear, courteous, hearty Kinsman Mr. Coney, where I am intimately acquainted, and frequently and splendidly Entertained, there are many Services to be done for the Souls of old and young. I need not insert here the partic-

---

[32] "The reference is to the difficulties between the town and the Reverend Benjamin Woodbridge, which up to his death in 1710 prevented the regular settling of a church" (Forbes). On May 19, 1712 the town invited Mr. Aaron Porter (H.C. 1708) to settle there as its minister, and on February 11 of the following year, Sewall records his ordination (*Diary*, II, 370). I am unable to identify the "Obstreperous person" or to explain the tantalizing monetary reference. See James M. Usher, *History of the Town of Medford* (Boston, 1886), pp. 222–24.

[33] Wooster.

ular Services I may design, but I shall be perpetually contriving what I may do for them according to their several Circumstances; never go anear them, without some Explicit Contrivance to do good among them.

4.G.D. I would make the present aspect of the Times an Engine to Serve the Cause of Piety. I would inculcate the Maxims and Methods of Piety with Powerful Considerations, drawn from the Times into which we are fallen. These considerations I would Exhibit and Inculcate, not only on the Lords-Days, but in my Lectures, and both in my Prayers and in my Sermons. I may contribute much unto the Goodness and wisdom of this whole people, by my being Awake on this Occasion.

5.G.D. In the *Society for the Suppression of Disorders,* I would move Some Special Methods to Preserve and Strengthen the *Religion of the Sabbath.*

6.G.D. Some Children in my Neighbourhood, are falling into a way of Wickedness, for which they must have Speedy Correction, and from which, a Speedy Recovery. I am to take some Care about them.

7.G.D. Among the Occasions for Expressions of Piety and Thankfulness, I would most affectionately take Notice of One that often occurs to me, in the mean Employments, wherein I see many other people occupied. When I see those whose business is, to Dig in the Earth, to Cleanse the Kennels, to Sweep the Chimneys, to drive the Wheel-barrows, and Carry Burdens, or the Like Things; of a Very Low Degree; I would have my Heart raised in Praises and Wonders, for the Sovereign Grace of God, which has distinguished me with much nobler and higher Employments; indeed, the best of all Employments. I would also Lift up a Prayer for the Neighbours which I see more meanly Employed; that God would help them to do what they do, out of Obedience unto Him; and also Bestow upon them Some Suitable Blessing, which I may be Led from the Circumstances of what I see them a doing, to think upon.

1.G.D. During the time of the Baptism, and the Ensuing Collections, many Children get out of the Assembly, and are abroad at play, Profaning the Sabbath, and Offending the People of God. I would use my Particular Endeavours to Prevent these Disorders. And all others, that I find the Children of the Flock to fall into.

2.G.D. My Children that have begun to handle their Pens, I will Oblige to Write an Answer to that Question; *What should be the Conduct of Baptized Children? What is the Duty their Baptism does oblige them to?* From their own Written Answer to this Question, I will take Occasion in the most Lively manner, to inculcate the Admonitions of Piety upon them.

3.G.D. To my aged Mother, I must present my, *Awakening Thoughts on the Sleep of Death,* and the Description of our Virtuous Aged Women, which is in the Preface; and accompany the Same with agreeable Passages of Conversation.[34]

4.G.D. I would wade as far as I can, in the Matter of Gathering a Church at *Rhode-Island,* and forward it, if it be Possible.

5.G.D. Some Very Pious, Generous, Liberal People in my Neighbourhood, have Lately received a Mercy in their Family, by the Safe Return of an only Son from Sea. I would Put them upon doing some Special Service for Christ, as an Expression of their Gratitude for Such a Mercy.

6.G.D. I think, I may do well, to take a List of Souls in my Flock, whom I know, or hear, or fear, to be remarkably Ensnared in Evil Courses, and Suitably and Solemnly apply myself, or procure Convenient Applications of others to be made, unto them that they may, if possible, be recovered.

25.d 2.m Friday.

This day I set apart for Prayer with Fasting before the Lord, and Such Alms as were proper for the Day. The Occasions were such

---

[34] Mrs. Maria (Cotton) Mather (1641–1714) married Increase Mather on March 6, 1662. Her father was the "celebrated" Mr. John Cotton (1584–1652) in whose honor Cotton Mather was named.

as are usual with me. But besides these, there were Some Special Errands to Heaven, in and for which I was concerned.

One was, to obtain Such an operation from the Spirit and Power of the Lord, as might allay, quiet, and compose, the Senseless Disturbance in our Angry Neighbourhood; at the Providing of New Seats in our Meeting house, for our Numerous Congregation. I Left this matter with Him who Stills the Raging of the Sea, and the madness of the People.

But then there was another Case, which I Endeavoured to Spread before the Lord.

An horrid Fellow, who is One of the Wickedest of Men, formerly made me the object of his malice, and his fury, and his Libels. He has Lately Endeavoured a Cursed Slander, and a Subornation of Mischief, against a Pious and faithful Magistrate, my very Good Friend Mr. *Bromfield*.[35] The Wretch goes on with Such boisterous Pride, and Mischievous Wickedness and Restlessness, that it appeared unto me, Time for us to carry him unto the Lord, with *United Supplications,* under the Encouragement of that word; *If two of you agree, touching any thing they shall ask, it shall be done for them.* Accordingly, that Gentleman, at my desire, joined with me, in part of the Duties of this Day. Having him with me in my Study, We together Entered before the Lord, our Complaint Concerning that Child of Belial. We first, Forgave him, and renounced with Abhorrence all Thoughts of a personal Revenge upon him. We asked the Lord also to Forgive him, and make him a New Creature, and bring him to the Tempers and Actions of Goodness, and that he might Share with us in all the Blessings of Goodness. But Yet we asked, that he might be Stopped in the per-

---

[35] Edward Bromfield (1649–1734), Mather's long-time friend and literary patron, was a member of the South Church and, in Sewall's words (*Letter-Book,* I, 224), a merchant "well known here and in England." Some eleven years earlier he had been instrumental in arranging for the publication of Mather's greatest work, the *Magnalia Christi Americana.* See Mather's entry for June 13, 1701 (*Diary,* I, 400), and Chester N. Greenough, "A Letter relating to the Publication of Cotton Mather's *Magnalia," Publications of the Colonial Society of Massachusetts,* XXVI (Jan. 1926), 296–312.

verse way, wherein he is going on before the Lord. We declared, how glad we should be, if he may be Stopped by a true Conversion. But if this might not be granted, We Entreated, that our Glorious and Enthroned JESUS, who has all Angels at his Command, would in His own Time, and His own Way, interpose, for our Deliverance from that persecutor, against whom, if he turn not, there are Arrows ordained; and with a Testimony that He does own us as His Poor Servants, I Considered what is done unto us. Particularly, we requested that the Guilty Monster may be Stricken with some sense of his Guilt, and Smitten with such a Remorse and Horror of Conscience, as may be a Warning unto other people, to take heed of those Impieties for which he has been so Exemplary.[36] We then Resolved, that by Way of Thankfulness to our Great Redeemer, for pleading our Cause, we would Endeavour Some Special Service to the Interests of Piety in the Country.

7.G.D. I Still find, that notwithstanding the Plentiful Provision I have made of Methods to Employ the Little Interstices of my Time unto the best of Purposes, Yet I am Still Unhappy, with many Minutes wherein my mind Lies wholly fallow, and is not Employed in any Acknowledgments of God, and of His Glorious Truths. I would therefore become furnished, with Proper Subjects; and make it my Practice, when I find myself in danger of Idle Minutes, then to form a Meditation on one or other of the Subjects, in such a method, as I anciently prescribed for Carrying on the Exercise of Meditation.

1.G.D. A Pious Young Man belonging to our Church, and my Brother-in-Law, (*Peter Oliver*) died this Morning. A few Hours before he died, he once and again importuned me, that I would Earnestly Exhort the Young People of the Place mightily to maintain and practice the Religion of the Closet; [37] unto which he said, through the Favour of God, he had not been himself a Stranger, but had found Unspeakable Advantage and Comfort

---

[36] This passage typifies Mather's "forgiveness" of his "Contemptible Enemies."
[37] See p. 40 (June 3).

in it. For me to take this Advantage, May be a great Service to the Interests of Piety in the Neighbourhood. And, I propose, with the Help of Heaven, on the next Lords-Day to do it.

27.d 2.m Lords Day.

Besides the other Intentions of being there, I Pursued more particularly these two Errands at the Table of the Lord.

The first was, that with every other Grace of the Holy Spirit, I may especially receive that Grace, of an Heart very Attentive to the worship of God, when I am to be Engaged in it.

The Second was, that if there be any one discriminating Point, which may keep upon me the Character of a Tare in the Field of the Lord, He would Please to Discover it to me, and Deliver me from it.

2.**G.D.** My Children are sensibly affected with the Death of their Uncle, in whose House, (which was next unto mine) they were daily Conversant. His Dying Desire, to have the prayer of the Closet recommended unto young People, gives me a Notable Engine to inculcate that grand Exercise of Religion, and Vehicle of all Good, upon them. I will improve it accordingly.

3.**G.D.** To my aged Aunt, at *Northampton,* I would send my Character of our Virtuous and Excellent Matrons, in the Preface to the Book more than once already mentioned; and some other Engines of Piety, to ripen her for the Heavenly World.[38]

4.**G.D.** I would write away unto the distressed Church at *Woodbridge,* My Directions, about supplying themselves with a desirable Minister.[39]

5.**G.D.** I must Renew my Proposal, for some Good Men to walk

[38] Mrs. Solomon Stoddard, whose former husband the Rev. Eleazar Mather (1637–1669), Increase Mather's brother, was Stoddard's predecessor at Northampton. The "aged Aunt" was not to die for yet another twenty-four years.

[39] Mr. Shipton states that in 1712 "Cotton Mather recommended [Samuel Wiswall (H.C. 1701)] for the pulpit at Woodbridge, New Jersey, from which Nathaniel Wade (Class of 1693) had been dismissed for 'grievous scandals,' but apparently the congregation had had enough of Harvard men" (Sibley, V, 127).

the streets in Evenings, where our Children are at play, and observe the Language of the Children, and take a Proper Notice of the Children who use any Wicked Language, and, if it be Possible, Reform their Wickedness. It grows at such a rate, that it is high time something were done for the suppression of it.

6.G.D. There is a poor person in my Neighbourhood, whom I would assist by sending in Something to furnish her, for the Beginning of House-keeping. I Suppose, the Great Quantity of Wine made by our Saviour, for the new-married Couple at *Cana*, was, that they might sell some of it, for the assistance of their Expenses, at their Beginning of House-keeping.

7.G.D. I live in a Neighbourhood, that seems full of Uncivil, Uncourteous, Unthankful, Unhelpful, Disobliging People. I have a frequent Experience of the Indisposition of the more boorish and sordid crew among them to treat me with Common Humanity. This furnishes me with an Opportunity to Imitate my Glorious Lord, and Exercise a Little of His Grace. When I meet with any absurd People, I would think, *What were the Duty that I should do or owe to these People, if they were ten times more obliging than they are?* And then Study and Essay, that I may not fail in my Duty to them, however they fail in theirs to me.

1.G.D. I have in my View, Several hopeful Essays, to bespeak and promote Early Piety among the Young People of the Flock; and I would, with much Supplication to Heaven, for Direction and Assistance therein, apply myself unto them.

2.G.D. There are some Exercises of Religion in my Family, which my Wife is Capable of Upholding and Cherishing; especially on the Saturday-Evenings, and the Lords-day Noons and Evenings; and I would prevail with her, to do her part in Carrying my Family to God, by such Pious Exercises.

3.G.D. I have some Kindred at *New Haven*, of whom I would this Day take a Particular Notice, with sending Books of Piety unto them.

4.G.D. It may have a Tendency further to advance Piety in the Country, if I give the Public, in the way of the Press, the Sermon I have newly preached at the Desire of my Deceased Brother-in-Law.

5.G.D. There are diverse Ministers in this Town, whom I may do well to put upon Discoursing with Several People in their Flocks, about the Miscarriages, and the Afflictions, and the various Temptations, under which I know them to be suffering.

6.G.D. There is an hopeful Young Man, proposed for an usher in the Grammar-school of this Town; for whom it would be a Considerable Kindness, if I could prevail with some Family of good Fashion, to give him his Board, and Entertain him, for the Exercises of Religion, with which he would accommodate them.

7.G.D. For the Recovery of my impaired Health, I must now and then take an Horse, and Ride a few Miles out of Town. I would make this an Opportunity, of acknowledging my dear Saviour, as the Lord of my Health, and of all the Creatures that serve me; and of Enriching the minds of the gentlemen who shall attend me in these Little Excursions, with as many Admonitions of Piety, and Useful Conversation, as may be.

III.) About this time, I sent unto the Press, a Book Entitled: PASTORAL DESIRES, *A short Catalogue of Excellent Things, which a True Pastor, will Desire to see Approved, and Practiced, and Abounding, among his People. A Book designed to be Lodged and Left in their Hands, by One Desirous to be such an One, in his Pastoral Visits, to the Houses of all his People.* In the Title, I have already Expressed, my Intention, in the Book thus published. I intend also, to send it, as fast as I can, into Every Town throughout the Country.

1.G.D. I can't instruct my Flock in a point of more general Usefulness unto them than the Methods of *Casting our Burdens on the Lord.* I would therefore discourse on that point unto them. And I would not only in handling this Matter, but also in other Essays of my Ministry, frequently Conclude my Sermons, with Culling out Work to be attended by my Hearers, in the following Evening. If this be done in a Lively and Cogent Manner, many Intentions of Piety will be served; Especially that of Well-spending the Lords-Day Evening.

2.**G.D.** The Health of the Several Children must be Looked after. And I would Contrive an Admonition of Piety for Each of them, relating to something in their Hearts and Lives analogous to the Bodily Distempers, against which I am now fortifying of them.

3.**G.D.** What shall be done for my Kinswoman come to Live at *Brookline?* [40] I must Endeavour in all the Ways I can imagine, to do Good unto her, and unto her Family.

4.**G.D.** It may be a Service to the Interests of Religion, and a thing Well-becoming a Minister of God, if I should give the Town a Lecture, to Encourage that Good Work of Building, which they are now much upon; and direct and bespeak the Acknowledgments wherewith God is to be glorified in it.[41]

5.**G.D.** I would not only Preach to the Societies of Young People, who are another generation Coming on, the Reason they have to beware of being another generation; but I would also very particularly and importunately Set before them the points

[40] This "Kinswoman," identified more specifically by the entry for September 23 (p. 78), was Ann (Lake) Cotton whose first husband John Cotton, minister of Hampton, New Hampshire (H.C. 1678), had died in 1710. In 1715 she became the second wife of Cotton Mather's father Increase whom she survived by fourteen years.

[41] The sermon Mather delivered on the day following that of this entry was concerned with the reconstruction of various buildings destroyed by Boston's "great fire" of Oct. 2, 1711. See Mather's comments on his sermons of 15.d 3.m (p. 128) and 2.d' 8.m (p. 131).

On April 25 the South Church had selected Joseph Sewall to join the Rev. Ebenezer Pemberton as its second minister. Samuel Sewall's comment (*Diary* II, 348) on Mather's failure to mention the selection lays bare one side of the strained New England sensibility. "Fifth day, May. 15th. Dr. Cotton Mather preaches from PS. 51. 18. Build thou the Walls of Jerusalem. . . . I could not perceive that in either of his prayers he did one jot mention the Building the South-church has in Hand in Settling another Minister. Let the gracious GOD be in the way, to be found, Near at hand; And even be found before we Seek, Hear before we call! Let the Bountifully Gracious GOD take away the filthy Garments from me, and from my Son, and give us Change of Raiment."

of their Danger. And, if I can get opportunity, I would extend these Admonitions further throughout the Country.

6.G.D. A Knight with whom I am intimately acquainted, has met with Great and Sore Troubles, and is at this time Exercised with some Domestic Encumbrances that are very grievous ones. I would Endeavour in all the ways imaginable, to Comfort him, and assist him, and Make his afflictive Circumstances, profitable to him. [Sir C.H.] [42]

7.G.D. I would Exceedingly improve in two points of Piety, relating to the Government of my Thoughts. The One is, that as Often as I find any Ill Thought shaping in my Mind, I will Rebuke it, I will Destroy it, with a Good one. It shall provoke me to shape a Good one; and this as much as may be, directly opposed unto the Ill Thought which would have infected me. The Other is; that I will frequently Reflect on the Condition and Employment of my Mind, and if I perceive no Tendency to a good Thought in the Operations of it, I will be angry with myself, and Labour to form some good Thought immediately. The Apprehension of having my Heart always under the View of the glorious God, and the Thoughts thereof afar off known unto Him, Exceedingly Quickens me, and Comforts me, in these Exercises of Piety: And the Thoughts which I therein fly unto, shall ordinarily be put into the Form of an Address unto the Lord, who Considers my meditation.

1.G.D. A Kind Present Lately Made unto me, for the Nourishment of the Children in my Family, has Awakened me, no Longer to delay my Purposes, to set anew upon the Exercise of

[42] Sir Charles Hobby, Colonel and senior officer at the capture of Port Royal on Oct. 2, 1710. Mather for a number of years had maneuvered ineffectually to have Sir Charles replace Governor Dudley, whom Mather detested. See for instance, Holmes, I, 247 and 256–57; *Diary,* I, 508 and II, 293; Thomas Hutchinson, *The History of the Colony of Massachusetts-Bay,* ed. Laurence Shaw Mayo (Cambridge, 1936), II, 114 and 130. Hutchinson wittily remarks that Hobby, whom he calls "a gay man [and] free liver," "had been knighted as some said for fortitude and resolution at the time of the earthquake in Jamaica, others for the further consideration of £800 sterling" (II, 114). In general, Hobby seems to have been not unencumbered with the imperfections attributed by Mather, with some justice, to Dudley.

Catechizing the Children in my Flock. Wherefore, I would this very week set upon it, and cry to the Glorious Lord for His Assistance in it and take the best Measures for the agreeable performance of it.

2.**G.D.** Among the Returns which I would make to the Glorious Lord, for His Blessings on my Family, I would set myself with more than ordinary Cogency, to have all Domestic Encumbrances and Avocations over, Every Saturday Evening, long before it be dark, that so the whole Family may have nothing to do, but apply themselves to Devotionary Exercises, and that the Lords-day may be duly prepared for.

3.**G.D.** I have two Sisters-in-Law, the One a Widow, the Other Languishing under sickness; to whom I owe a Various Duty.

4.**G.D.** The Time draws near, for the Anniversary Convention of our Ministers; I would set myself to Contrive the most Edifying Entertainment for them. I would Entertain them with such subjects of Discourse as may be for the General Advantage. I would set forward such things among them as all the Country may fare the better for.

One thing that I propose to Exhibit unto them, is, A Catalogue of *Evil Customs* which begin to appear in the Country, and *Proper Methods* to discourage them. I would ask them to Concur in Exhibiting it unto the Country; and to Complete it by their own Communications for that Purpose.

5.**G.D.** Fresh occasions occur, for me to animate a Minister in our Vicinity, to write a brief Treatise, which he has been disposed and preparing to write, in the defense of our ordination, to stop the Mouths of the High-flying Party,[43] who are very Venomous and Mischievous, in some of our Southern Colonies.

6.**G.D.** There is a Religious and well-disposed Candidate of the Ministry, who has met with Discouragements, and is out of Employment. I would immediately apply myself to find some Good Employment for him. [$^{c}a\lambda\epsilon$] [44]

[43] Advocates and members of the Church of England.   [44] Hale.

23.d 3.m Friday.

I Set apart this Day, for Prayers with Fasting before the Lord, on Such Occasions, as employed me this Day a month ago.[45]

And as then, so now, I had my Pious Friend Mr. *Bromfield* with me, in some of the Sacrifices.

7.G.D. I am desirous to take a Catalogue of the Comforts which I do at this time Enjoy; and Employ this Thought upon Each of them, *What Special Service to my dear Saviour, does this Favour of His unto me, most agreeably Call me to?* And the Comforts that may in the Time to Come arrive unto me, I would Entertain with the Like Thoughts upon them.

1.G.D. Having Entered upon the Stroke of *Catechizing,* and this with very Encouraging Circumstances, I find beginning to appear already a world of precious Opportunities to Do Good among the Young ones in the Neighbourhood. I would cry to Heaven for assistance, and use all Possible Contrivance and Diligence, in Cultivating these Opportunities. And Particularly, I would proceed now, to think on the best Methods, that the Daughters of our *Zion* may come into them.

25.d 3.m Lords Day.

My Errands to the Table of the Lord were these.

First, Giving Thanks to the Gracious God, for planting me in His House, I did what I could, with a Consenting Soul, that I might be united unto the glorious JESUS, as the Root from whence I Expected all Saving Influences. I then Considered my Jesus, as Purchasing, and as Dispensing, the Grace that should Cause me to Flourish in the House of God. And so I went on to Specify the Particular Articles, wherein I requested of Him, and relied on Him, to make me Flourish there; Especially, in the Con-

---

[45] See pp. 29 and 51.

tinual Exercise of Grace; and in Writing those things that will be Abiding Fruits among His people.

Next. I beheld the Blood of my Glorious Jesus, as purchasing all Needful Grace for me; and I discerned, that I needed abundance of Grace, in regard of my Relations, Conditions, Temptations, Employments, and the Services that were Expected from me. I took the Sacred Cup, as a Pledge of that Grace; and then I Signed unto the Lord my Expectations of it. But I Singled out Especially Two Points, Wherein I Wished that I might be Supplied with it. First; Grace to prosecute the Religious and Excellent Education of my Family. Secondly. Grace not only to Contrive Exquisite Methods of Piety, but also to Perform them; and to Execute the precious Resolutions, which from time to time I am led unto.

2.**G.D.** The next Addition to the Evening Sacrifices in my Family, I propose to be, a Recitation to be made by the Several Children, of, *The Body of Divinity Versified*.[46] Whereof, I would Still Open and Apply a Distich at a time, till we are got through it.

3.**G.D.** I have some Kinsmen in the Indian Service, and would animate them to study and contrive all the ways imaginable, for the promoting of Christianity among the Indians.

4.**G.D.** I may have an opportunity with the Ministers of the Province, at their Convention, to do many Services, of an Extended Consequence. Among others, this may be one; to make them apprised of the Condition of Religion, and of the Church abroad in the world.

Another shall be, to awaken in them a Concern to rescue our Frontiers, from the Vices that Strangely grow upon them.

5.**G.D.** I would join with the Ministers of the Province in an Address unto the Society for the Propagation of Religion, Re-

[46] Mather's summation of Christian doctrine in twenty-seven rhyming couplets did not appear as a separate publication. It made up a part of various such catechistic books as *Maschil* (1702), in which, Holmes suggests, it might first have seen print.

monstrating the Mischiefs done by their Missionaries in these parts of the world.[47]

6.G.D. There is an aged Minister, twenty miles to the Southward, Conflicting sometimes with difficult Circumstances. I will send some Supplies unto him.

7.G.D. I find myself still at some times Exceedingly defective in this point; When some sort of Troublesome Occurrences arise; Especially in the foolish and froward Humours of Discontented People, I can't Sufficiently preserve that Sedate, and Serene, and Comfortable Frame of Mind which belongs unto the *Peace of God.* I would fain grow more Expert at the Piety, whereof I find in myself Such Deficiency. I would particularly thus Exercise it. On any Trouble that arises, I would presently find out, and fly to, a Promise in the Covenant of God, that may answer unto it. I would behold the Blessed Jesus, as Purchasing for me all the Good of that Promise; and as being able from the Throne of God whereon He sits, attended with the Hosts of Heaven, to accomplish it all. I would then cast upon Him all the Care of a Good Issue of the Trouble; and also Look up unto Him to Quiet and Compose my Mind, and give me that Rest which He has promised unto them that come unto Him.

In this Matter, I would observe; that the more than ordinary Disturbance of Mind which sometimes is raised in me, seems from some Circumstances to arise very much from a Satanic Energy; from some Violent and furious Temptation of Satan. I would therefore on those Occasions, Cry to my dear and great Saviour, most Explicitly, that the Enemy may be restrained, and the Devil rated off.

1.G.D. An Exquisite Prudence, and Patience, and Contrivance with Applications to Heaven and Earth, is necessary, to conquer the Temptations of Satan, and to defeat His Devices against the Flock, in some Disturbance of Mind, occasioned by the building

---

[47] See pp. 21 and 45.

of some New Seats in our Meeting-house. I would on this occasion Endeavour such a Conduct as may have a Tendency to bruise Satan under our feet.

2.**G.D.** My Children which go to Schools, have their Holidays. These Holidays devoted Entirely to play, have a tendency to deprave their Minds, and bring a sickly Frame upon them. I would therefore, when these Holidays arrive, take Special Care, that they Learn some Good Thing in the morning at home, and (such of them as are able to do it) Write something that I shall assign them, for their Instruction and Improvement in Piety.

3.**G.D.** I am in conversation with my Kinsman, the Minister at *Saybrook;* [48] and there are several services to the Kingdom of God, wherein I am Engaging and Assisting of him.

About this time I have another Little Book in the Press. It is the Sermon preached at the Death and the Desire of my Brother-in-

(IV.) Law. The Title is: THE YOUNG MAN SPOKEN TO. *Another Essay to Recommend and Inculcate the Maxims of Early Religion unto Young Persons; and Especially the Religion of the Closet. In a Sermon Preached unto them, on a Special Occasion.*

4.**G.D.** In a Town of Good people, thirty miles off, they are sorely Visited with Agues. I would Send Advice and Relief unto them.

I would Procure an Authentic Relation of the Unaccountable Proceedings of the wretched Company who pretend for the Ch. of E. at *Newbury;* the Publication whereof may be a great Service to the Interests of Religion.

5.**G.D.** I would accompany the Ministers of the Town, and with them go to both Houses in the General Assembly, and with a Presentation of our Memorial Speak to them as Prudently, but as Pungently as I can, upon the points contained in it.

6.**G.D.** There is a Poor Man of my Flock, who has Lain under Long Languishments, and perhaps Necessities may grow upon him. I must Visit him, and Comfort him, and see what Reliefs may be necessary for him. [Φαυκs] [49]

7.**G.D.** As I would Look back on the Books I have heretofore pub-

[48] Azariah Mather. See p. 5, n. 3.   [49] Fawkes.

lished, with sollicitous Endeavours, that my Heart and Life may be Conformed unto all the Maxims of Piety, which I inculcate upon other people, so whatever I now publish, I would with much attention peruse and ponder Every Article of it, and compare myself with it, and be Exceedingly sollicitous that nothing I have written may prove my own condemnation.

1.G.D. My Book of *Pastoral Desires* is now got through the Press. And now, with many and ardent Cries to the Glorious Lord for His Assistances, I would set Myself to Visit all the Families of the Numerous Flock; and with all possible Solemnity dispense the suitable Admonitions of Piety unto all sorts of persons in them. And then Leave the Book in Each of the Families, with my Request, that Every Person therein may peruse it, and partake of his own portion in it.

2.G.D. My Son *Increase* is now got so forward, that I May Maintain my daily discourse with him wholly in the Latin Tongue. Such a practice, taken up, would be of great use to both of us.

3.G.D. Some Circumstances in the State of my Sister *Abi's* Health,[50] oblige me to treat her with some singular Essays of preparation for the Heavenly world; which I will now Endeavour accordingly.

4.G.D. It would be an Excellent Service unto the Churches of God, and Especially unto ours in these Colonies if the Superstitions and Iniquities in the Ch. of E. were truly and fairly Exhibited, and in a brief, Comprehensive, but yet Intelligible Representation of them. I would, as soon as I can, Endeavour it.

5.G.D. I would present unto the Society for Suppression of Disorders, my Catalogue of *Evil Customs,* and propose the publication thereof unto the Country.

6.G.D. There is in My Neighbourhood a Family of Motherless, Miserable, Uncultivated Children. Immediate Care must be taken, to have them well-disposed of.

7.G.D. I am now Entering into the Summer. The Wishes and

---

[50] His sister Abigail, born in 1677, lived until 1748, surviving her elder brother by twenty years.

Prayers whereto I am to be awakened from the Circumstances of the Summer, are now seasonable to be used, both privately and publicly. They are at the End of this Book.[51]

1.G.D. In Visiting the Families of the Flock, I would particularly insist on these points of Inquiry and Instruction.

First. The Grand Concern of getting into Good Terms with Heaven, by Speedy Repentance, Through Conversion.

Secondly. The Family-Sacrifice, as well as the Religion of the Closet.

Thirdly. The Education of the Children.

Fourthly. The best way of Spending the Lords-day-Evening. Many other Subjects will occur, as I see Occasion.

Especially this; What Affliction they meet with, and what Good they get by it.

And I would not be discouraged by any Bad Usage in the Flock, from going through my Duty, and Overcoming Evil with Good.

2.G.D. Inculcating on my Children the Methods, by which they are to get into Good Terms with Heaven, I would pathetically manage this Argument with them. Doubtless, I am quickly to Die and Leave them. And I must Leave them in an ungrateful and barbarous world, where my Testimonies for Piety have procured me many Enemies. If they have not God for their Friend, if their Saviour be not Singularly Concerned for their welfare, what will become of them?

3.G.D. It seems a seasonable Duty and Service, for me to Comfort and Hearten and Encourage my Aged Parent; Especially with regard unto his Usefulness among the people, and their Affection unto him. And observe the points, wherein he may be most Likely to give way unto Discouragement; and obviate them, that he may Enjoy a Joyful as well as a Fruitful Old Age.

4.G.D. The Condition of the Church at *Norwich*, which is by some of the Brethren there, Laid before me, Calls for some

[51] See *"Desideria Vernalia," "Desideria Æstivalia," "Desideria Autumnalia,"* pp. 124–25, and p. 17, n. 24.

Exquisite and Laborious Endeavours in me to help them; to which I am applying myself accordingly.[52]

5.G.D. In my Pastoral Visits, I would make the Growth of the Religious Societies, One Article of my Conversation with the Neighbourhood. In Conversing with such as belong to the Societies, I would Enquire into the Circumstances of the Societies, and Consult and Concert with them, how to recruit them, and quicken the Exercises of Piety in them. In Conversing with such as yet belong to none, I would put them where I see them fit for it, upon joining themselves, where they may be benefited.

6.G.D. A Fatherless Child, is become a Servant in my Family. There shall be Kindnesses, which I will dispense unto him, as an Orphan.

20.d 4.m Friday.

I set apart this Day for Prayers and Alms, with Fasting before the Lord. Besides the more usual Occasions and Exercises for such a Day, wherein I was now Concerned, there were Some Special Things, which Employed my Supplications.

I have Several important Services before me, for which I need the Special Direction and Assistance of Heaven.

[52] The reference is to one of the nastier incidents in New England Church history. In 1708 the Rev. John Woodward (H.C. 1693), minister to the Church at Norwich, Connecticut, had acted as secretary to the synod which drew up the Saybrook Platform. Mr. Woodward's warm advocacy of the Platform encountered the equally warm opposition of his Church. The result was a "test case in the conflict between the older Congregationalism and the effort to stay the declining religious interest by the closer unity of the Saybrook Platform" (Sibley, IV, 187–88).

Eight years of bickering over ecclesiastical polity, on the one hand, and a proper ministerial salary (plus the payment thereof), on the other, culminated, on September 13, 1716, in "the dismission of Mr. Woodward"; a dismission "advised . . . as the only solution . . . by a council of the foremost ministers of New England." Mr. Shipton suggests the "hopelessness" of the situation by pointing out that after Mr. Woodward's departure the Norwich church splintered into seven separate congregations (*ibid.*).

In 1721, as a consequence of a legal judgment in his favor, the ousted minister finally received "the arrears of his salary." See also Frances M. Caulkins, *History of Norwich, Connecticut* (1866), pp. 284–85.

Moreover, On the Occasion of the Setting up of some New Pews in our Meeting-house, there has been a Strange Disturbance in the Minds of the People. And many of the Church have been Extremely Foolish and Froward. And they have, with much Injustice, made me the object of many Calumnies, for Permitting a thing which yet was not unreasonable. I now humbled and judged Myself before the Lord, for all the Miscarriages of my Conduct as a Pastor of the Flock, and pleaded the Great Sacrifice for my pardon. I then besought of Him who Stills the Raging of the Sea, that He would also quiet the Madness of the people; and Compose their tumultuous Disturbances. I went on, to pray, that the Lord would mercifully Forgive all their Murmurs against me in their Tents; and be Reconciled unto the Flock, and not be provoked by any of their Distempers, to break forth with His wrath against them; for which I also presented before the Lord, the Sacrifice for the Congregation.

7.**G.D.** This Morning My Mind runs much on the Vast Consequence of my assuring a claim to the Character of, *An Overcomer*. So I resolved on the Most Explicit methods of Listing myself under the Banner and Conduct of my admirable Saviour, and of obtaining His Assistances for all my Encounters. But it was herewithal my Resolution also, to keep a Watchful Eye on all my Sinful Inclinations; and Suppress and Subdue them still in all their Tendencies; as Particularly, Sloth, Pride, Lust, Wrath, Envy, and Worldly-Mindedness. And it was my Resolution Watchfully to mind all the Temptations that may be offered me, to desert any Good Cause, or befriend any Evil One; and Reject with abhorrence all the Motions of the Tempter to me. O Captain of my Salvation, Do Thou make me a Conqueror, and more than a Conqueror!

1.**G.D.** Considering the Evil Frame, in many of the Flock, and the Great Want of Brotherly-Love among them, I think, I may do well to play on *David's* Harp unto them, and preach them as Engaging a Sermon, as I can, on Rom. XII. 10: And at the same time set a Winning Example before them, and give a Description of Pastoral Love unto them, in such Strains, that the Conscience of the Hearers will tell them, 'tis no other than what they have seen Exemplified unto them. I would also bring them unto the Lords-Table as a Love-feast; and make it an Awakening Occasion to throw away all sour Leaven from among them.

22.d 4.m Lords Day.

My Essays at the Table of the Lord, were to Enkindle the Flames of Love in the first place, unto our Saviour, and then unto one another.

2.G.D. Now to Employ my Son *Increase* very frequently, in transcribing of such Instruments as may have a Tendency to inform his Mind and Manners, and requite him with a Supply of Money in his pocket, may Prove many ways advantageous to him.

3.G.D. A Family remotely related unto my Wife, is fallen into miserable Circumstances of Sin and Sorrow. This gives me an opportunity, to do many services, especially for the more Innocent and Suffering part of the poor Family.

4.G.D. There is a considerable Service before me; for which I must implore the Assistances of the glorious Lord. I am to draw up a Memorial, to be Laid before the English Society for Propagation of Religion, wherein I am to propose the Stopping of their Indirect Methods to deprave and molest Religion under the pretence of propagating it. This Memorial will require a very nice management.

5.G.D. The Prison in this place, (the Keepers House,) is a place of Tippling and Gaming, and horrible Disorders and Debaucheries. Wretched People and their Families, are hurried on to Ruin by that abominable House. I must concern myself, with the Society, or with the Justices, to get that Stumbling-block of Iniquity removed.[53]

[53] A proposal made at a meeting of "Free holders" (March 9, 1712/13) helps to identify the cause of the conditions to which Mather refers. "John George hath proposed to the Consideration of the Town Whether the Alms House ought not to

6.G.D. There is a Poor Aged Negro Woman, (yet a member of our Church) who must be provided for, and helped in her Needy Circumstances.

7.G.D. The Temptations that I Suffer from a very Humoursome and Ungrateful people ought to be wisely Encountered. I would think very much on the Conduct of the Patient JESUS. I would Keep a mighty Guard on my Language, that I may not Speak unadvisedly with my Lips. And I would be but the More useful to the people for their being Abusive to me. The Example of *Moses* and of *Paul,* would also Supply me with Excellent Considerations.

1.G.D. The *Catechizing Stroke* is a Part of my Ministry, which my Mind is much Set upon the fulfilling of. I am Seeking after *Witty Inventions,* for the more Profitable Management of it. I may, if the Lord Please, take an opportunity, here to insert Several of them. In the Meantime, I will advise with the Principal Persons in the Church, about the most agreeable Circumstances.

2.G.D. It Will be a Parental Fidelity in me, towards my Children, to Consider what are those Errors of the Wicked, and False Opinions in Religion, Which they may be in any Danger hereafter to be Led away withal; and in the most Exquisite Methods to Instruct them, and arm them, and warn them against those paths of the Destroyer. In the Saturday Evenings, I may have an opportunity to go through the Catalogue of the Errors, which are at this Day prevailing in the world.

3.G.D. To as many of my Relatives as I can, I would present my

---

be restored to its Primitive and Pious design, even for the relief of the necessitous, that they might Lead a quiet Peaceable and Godly life there, whereas 'tis now made a Bridewell and House of Correction, which Obstructs many Honest Poor People's going there for the designed Relief and Support. If therefore the Town would Lay out Some money, to the building a House of Correction in Some Other place, and refit the Alms House for the Comfortable reception of the distressed it will be a great Act of Charity" (*Report of the Record Commissioners,* XI [1884], 93). For the report of the Committee set up to consider this proposal, see *ibid.,* pp. 96–97.

Pastoral Desires; and therein Express my Concern to have them Holy and Happy.

4.**G.D.** I would greatly Unite my Studies with some Gentlemen, to Invent Methods, for the Defending of the College from Corruption, and the Rendering of it Useful to the Churches, and the Instilling of Good Principles into the Minds of the Students there.

Engage some of the hopeful Young Gentlemen there, to be better acquainted with me.[54]

5.**G.D.** I am advised, that writing a Letter unto a Neighbour town, may produce a Revival of Religious Societies there. I would at a fit season Endeavour it.

6.**G.D.** The Godly Minister of *Quoboag*,[55] is in Mean and Low Circumstances. It will be a good work to comfort him, in his dangerous and difficult Circumstances. I will not only myself dispense Reliefs unto him, but also procure some from others.

A Young Man, a Stranger, and a Captive is this Week dying here. Not only my Visits, but my Disbursements are needful on this occasion; and my Letters of Comfort unto his parents.

A Worthy Family in my Neighbourhood is brought into Extreme and Wondrous Distress, by the Secret Malice of some Wicked People. I can, and will, do more, than any man alive, to deliver them; and I Would make it also an occasion to promote Piety in them.[56]

7.**G.D.** My Gracious and Glorious Lord, in answer to my impor-

---

[54] On this day (July 2) Mather attended commencement exercises at Harvard College. The corresponding entry in Sewall reflects rather neatly some of the many ways in which his personality and his *Diary* differ significantly from Mather's: "Went with Mr. Hall to the commencement; at Charlestown fell in with Dr. Cotton Mather, went above a Mile before we got a Calash, and then paid full price" (II, 354).

[55] Quoboag, Mass., now Brookfield, where "in the spring of 1711 [Mr. John James] began to preach . . . and to enjoy the 20 £ a year with which Massachusetts subsidized the minister[s]" of this little frontier outpost so often ravaged by the Indians (Sibley, V, 16).

[56] This passage is written in the margin opposite the entry for July 4.

tunate Cries unto Him, has given me a Sweet Satisfaction of Mind, in His Truth, concerning Three Eternal Persons in His infinite Godhead; and a Victory over Temptations to Arianism, which have hideously assaulted and harassed my Mind. By way of Thankfulness to the Lord, I would now practically more than ever Converse with that mystery, in my daily Supplications and Dependences; And Study ways also to Strengthen my Brethren.

1.G.D. I Lately declared in a Sermon, that God would Speedily take Some of our young Men, and make them dreadful Examples of His Wrath, and hang them up in Chains for all the Congregation of our Israel to tremble at. And the Last Lords Day, I declared, that I Lived in a daily and a trembling Expectation, of what the Lord would Speedily do upon Some among them. And Lo, this Last week, 'tis come to pass. A knot of our poor young men, are detected in horrid Burglaries. They are brought out, and become fearful Examples of Sin and Punishment. I would make this an occasion, and it is indeed a very Pungent one, to Renew my Warnings unto the Rising Generation.

2.G.D. The Admission of my Son *Increase* into the College, is now proposed. This brings an occasion of much Prayer to God; and much Advice to the Child.

3.G.D. I have some Relatives, the Children of my Cousin-Germans, in the Colony of *Connecticut*, unto whom I do not remember that I have yet sent any Expressions of my concern for their Welfare. I will now by the mediation of my Kinsman at *Saybrook*, find them out, and address them with Books of Piety.

4.G.D. From the Southward, I am addressed with a Desire, to Publish Something that may be an Antidote against Antinomian Errors, which are an occasion of much Mischief among the People there. I would, as soon as I can, Endeavour it.[57]

5.G.D. On the occasion of the Late Robberies and Outrages Committed by our Children, as I would myself Make a seasonable and agreeable Discourse at the Lecture, so I would Stir up the

[57] See p. 119, n. 35.

other Ministers, to bear their Testimonies, and Warn the Young People of the Town against the Way of Transgressors.

6.G.D. There is a Number of Distracted People, that fall under my Cognizance. They and their Families are objects of much Compassion. I will do what I can for them.

7.G.D. I Must carefully Examine my Large Library, and see whether I may have Lying there any Books unduly detained from the true owners of them and make a Speedy Restitution. 'Tis what I have newly been Pressing in the Public Exhortations. Oh! What shall [I] render to my Glorious Lord! Oh! how shall I Love Him, and Praise Him, and Serve Him! He deals marvelously with me, He will go on, after an astonishing Manner, to make use of me, in Service for Him. I had nothing that Lay ready to be Published and dispersed among the People of God. I thought, my Glorious Lord Will Provide work for me, and such pieces of work, as I have the Least foresight of. So it falls out. A Number of Wicked Young Men in the Town, have made themselves a Band of Robbers. The Holy God has discovered them. The Town and Land is full of Discourse on the occasion. It furnishes me with an Opportunity, to Speak Some things of great Importance unto the Manners of the People, and especially to dispense Admonitions of Piety, to our Young People, and Solemn and Pungent Warnings against the Courses of Dishonesty. A Vast Assembly Came together at the Lecture. I prepared for it, under the Conduct of God, and His Good Angel, in all the Circumstances of my Study. I Enjoyed a Mighty Assistance in the Preaching of it; the Word of God came with a mighty Energy. The Next Day, a Bookseller, from whom I Little Expected such a Matter, asked me for a Copy

(V.) of the Sermon. So it goes to the press, under this Title; A TRUE SURVEY AND REPORT OF THE ROAD. *A brief Essay to Rectify the Mistakes of Men, about the Way Chosen by them. The Whole Way of Transgression; and Particularly the Wrong Way, Wherein Men Transgress the Rules of Honesty Proved an Hard Way. And the Good Way of Religion therefore Preferred and Commended. In a Lecture at* Boston, *on a Special and Mournful Occasion.*

$$\frac{12.\text{d}}{13.\text{d}}$$ 5.m Saturday night.

I attended Something of a *Vigil*. I Sent up Nocturnal Cries unto the Lord, from the Dust, in which I Lay Prostrate before Him. I glorified Him with Raptures, for the Satisfaction He had given me in the Knowledge of His Name; in that He had Satisfied me in the Mystery of Three Persons in One God, the United Fountain of all Good. I Chose Him, even such a God, for my God. I begged this Favour of Him, that I may be Employed in Publishing the Praises of His Glorious Christ unto the World. And then there was another Favour which I begged of Him; This was, that I may understand the uniting Principles and Properties of that People, who are to be the Stone Cut out of the Mountains; and be improved in the Shaping and Serving of that Holy People, for the Grand Revolution that is now Coming on. There were other mercies for which I now also offered my Petitions.

1.**G.D.** Because One Young Man belonging to a Religious Society, has Lately proved an horrid Instance of Hypocrisy and Apostasy, there is a Strange Cry, raised among the Humorous People of the Town, to Put down all such Societies. That the Societies in my own Flock may not be discouraged on this occasion, I would both Publicly and Privately discourse at such a rate, as to defeat the force of the Temptation.

2.**G.D.** That God may bless me in my own Children, I would Labour in all the ways imaginable for the good of other Children. I would be Particularly Restless, until a more Effectual Provision be made, for the Restraint of our Children, Who profane the Sabbath and Service of God, by their public Misbehaviour in and near the Meeting-house.

3.**G.D.** I would take a particular Cognizance of a Little Kinsman at Charlestown, and bestow my counsels, with a Book, upon him.

4.**G.D.** The Time of Insupportable Heat, indisposes for Doing any thing of importance, and almost for Thinking. However, at this Time writing some Letters abroad, among other Services and Projections for the Kingdom of God, I propose unto Ministers, that they would at this Time Study Sermons on Such Subjects as a Glorious Christ affording the Shadow of a Great Rock in a weary Land; and find Something in the Time, to recommend Him unto their People.

5.**G.D.** The Commissioners for the Indian-affairs, are to meet this Day at my House. Among other Things to be pursued among them, one is, For some of us, to take a Journey unto *Natick,* and Endeavour a Cohabitation of Christian Indians there; under as good a Regulation as may be.

6.**G.D.** There are Miserables in the prison, whom I may do well to Visit, and Instruct; and also Relieve the wants, of some of them.

18.d 5.m Friday.

I set apart this Day, for the Devotions of a Fast in Secret before the Lord. The Occasions and Petitions, were of the Same Sort, with such as I use Every Month to bring and on my Knees. But Especially, I cried unto the Lord, that I might be directed and assisted in a great Intention, which I have now before me, to Exhibit the glories of my dear JESUS, as every Article of our Holy Religion invites us to take Notice of them.

I also Sought for a Smile of God, on a Journey to *Natick,* which I have the next week, with some other gentlemen, before me.

I had my Good Friend Mr. *Bromfield,* joining with me in Some of the Duties of this Day, Especially on the occasion formerly mentioned for our united Supplications. We have now *besought the Lord thrice* on that occasion.[58]

7.**G.D.** The Pagans of old, had their Several gods, for Various Benefits and Occasions. The Papists have their Saints, for the Like. I would, as soon as I can, Make a Collection of them; and

[58] See pp. 29 and 37 (April 25 and May 23).

then I would, in the most Explicit manner, find all in my Admirable JESUS, and give Him the Glory of blessing me with all Benefits, and on all Occasions.

1.**G.D.** I think, that, besides the Catechetical Exercises, which I Set up, for the Youth of the Neighbourhood, I must visit the Several Schools, where the Female and Lesser Children are together; that so I may Enlighten and Awaken them also with the most suitable Instructions for them.

20.d 5.m Lords Day.

My Errands to the Table of the Lord, were these Two, above the rest.

First, I considered the Glorious JESUS, having Purchased the Favours of God for me; and very particularly, one which I would reckon among the greatest Favours; that is, that He would show me His Glory. That I may be Enlightened and Satisfied in the Mystery of God manifest in Flesh. That since I am admitted unto so near a Communion with my Saviour; I may know, who He is. And, that His Good Spirit may help me to Learn from His Word, what Sort of a person He is; and by Consequence Lead me into Right Thoughts about the glorious and wonderful Doctrine of the Trinity. Some Circumstances and Temptations of the Day, Call me to be very sollicitous for the Divine Illuminations; which in this way I am Seeking for.

Secondly. And having some Special occasion to serve the Churches of God, by some Antidotes against Antinomian Errors,[59] I took the Like Method, for obtaining Instruction from Heaven, for that Purpose; and that the Doctrines of Grace may be clearly Revealed to me, rightly received by me. I considered my dear JESUS as the *Truth;* and as the Heavenly Teacher, who will Convey Truth unto them, who thus Look up unto Him for it.

2.**G.D.** I am often prescribing to my Children, the Rules of Good Manners. A Thought Comes into my Mind, that I may Suggest

[59] See p. 119, n. 35.

unto them Still Certain agreeable Maxims of Piety, on which those Rules may be practised, or at Least, with which they may be attended. I will make the Experiment.

3.**G.D.** Such of my Relatives as are employed in the Evangelical Service among the Indians, I would greatly animate unto an holy and lively Prosecution of it, and Procure them Encouragements in it.

22.d 5.m Tuesday.

Yesterday was a mighty Rain; all the Last Night was also Rainy, and this morning threatened the continuance of it. I was Engaged with some other gentlemen, the Indian Commissioners, in a Journey of Twenty Miles, unto *Natick,* that we may Inspect the Condition of the Christian Indians there, and Revive Religion, and Good Order among them, which have been under a grievous Decay.[60] We had appointed the Indians of some other Villages to meet us there, that we may propose unto them, a Removal for a Cohabitation there. I apprehended, that the Prince of the Power of the Air, who had been the Lord unto these Children of Disobedience, would, if possible, Get Leave, by a Long Storm, or some other Evil Accidents, to defeat our undertaking. But I considered

[60] Founded in 1651, Natick was the first and most important of John Eliot's settlements of Christian Indians. By 1712, partly as the result of the effects of King Philip's War on the Indian population, the decay of such "Praying Towns" was well-nigh complete. "The Number of *Indians* in the Land," states Mather, "is not comparable [in 1710] to what it was, in the . . . former Century" (*Bonifacius,* p. 195). And the death of Eliot in 1690 had been a disastrous blow to the cause. As Mather remarks elsewhere, "The Indian church at Natick . . . is, since blessed Eliot's death, much diminished and dwindled away" (Oliver N. Bacon, *A History of Natick* [Boston, 1856], p. 26).

A letter from William Ashhurst (Jan. 15, 1711/12) enumerates certain benefits to be hoped from a proper "Cohabitation": "to prevent the Indians being scattered up and down the Continent, and returning to the barbarous Customs of their Ancestors . . . [and to] . . . bring them to a sociable and civilized way of living after the European fashion [which] is the best way to engage them to the English interests and a good step towards making them Christians." By 1721 no trace of the original church at Natick was to be found (*ibid.,* pp. 21 and 61).

the Glorious JESUS, as a Superiour Lord, and as Him that has the Command of the Rain, the Wind, the Sun, and of all Creatures. I committed the whole Journey and all the Affair of it into His Glorious Hands; and with a Lively Faith, foresaw it would be a Journey of much Service and Comfort. We began our Journey this Morning; the Weather Soon cleared up; Every thing fell out agreeably. We arrived at *Natick,* Seasonably. A Considerable Congregation both of Indians and of English were come together there. The Minister whom we Expected, was not come. Wherefore, I did in my Extemporaneous Way, and with a very Singular Assistance from Heaven, Carry on the Exercises of Religion in their Meetinghouse. I Preached in their Pulpit, (without Bible, cushion, or Hour-glass) [61] a Sermon, first unto the Indians and then unto the English, on Act. 26. 18. After the Exercises were over, we discoursed with the Indians, about their Political Affairs. This being finished, we traveled unto *Sherburn;* where we were Comfortably Lodged. On Wednesday morning, we returned unto *Natick;* where the Worthy Minister, whom we Expected yesterday, Carried on the Exercises of Religion, in a Renewed Assembly of Indians, all in the Indian Language. We also renewed our Discourses with them, about their Interests; and Received handsome Returns of Thanks from them.

In the Evening, we arrived home, with Such Experience of the Divine Favour, that we were not able to Reflect on one uneasy Circumstance in all the Journey.[62]

4.**G.D.** A Dutch Minister, Come to *Albany,* is Willing to Serve the Interests of Religion among the *Iroquois* Indians. I would see what may be done for his Encouragement.

5.**G.D.** A worthy Minister, who was of the Same Class with me at the College, is a man of good, fine Abilities, Capable of doing

---

[61] Though lined out with a single stroke, the words within parentheses remain clearly legible.

[62] On July 22, Sewall notes only that "Dr. C. Mather, Sir Charles Hobby, Major Fitch and I set out for Natick. At Mills's the President [John Leverett, President of Harvard College] meets us, Fisher conducts us, Mr. Deming in company, Benj. Larnell waited on us. Murat was there with his trumpet" (II, 356).

many Services and Very ready to hearken to me. I would Cultivate a more free and frequent Correspondence with him, and
make it an Opportunity of putting him upon many Services.[63]

The Serenading Stroke is begun by some Lewd People among
us; and carried on with the Last Extremity of profaneness. A
Timely Stop should be put unto it.

6.G.D. My Late Sermon on the *Hard Way of the Transgressor* [64]
is Published. I would take some care, that particularly all the
Prentices on the Dock have it presented unto them.

7.G.D. My Slothfulness, My Slothfulness! the fearful Disease under
which I am Languishing! My Soul is Exceeding Sorrowful, in
the Sense of the Complicated Iniquity and Stupidity, which I
am therein guilty of; I am amazed at the Mischiefs which do
from thence arise unto me; What precious Opportunities to do
good and great Things, are therein Sinned away. What Shall I
do, for the Cure of this Malady. I will Cry mightily to my great
Saviour, that He would Cure it, by the Influences of His Holy
Spirit upon me. Yea, I would Set apart shortly a Whole Day, for
Cries unto the Lord, on this deplorable Occasion. And I would
bestow more Aculeating Rebukes than ever upon myself every
Evening, if the foregoing Day has not been Spent With a Comfortable Industry.

1.G.D. In my Numerous Flock, I am tried, with a very Froward,
Unkind, Ingrateful People. I am desirous, not only that none
of their Ill Usage may discourage me from a most Industrious
Discharge of my Duty towards the Flock; but I would also Use
the most Exquisite and Generous Contrivances I can imagine,
that I may overcome Evil with Good, and that I may in my Carriage to them have the Perfect Reverse of theirs to me. The more
backward they are to do any Good Offices for me, the Readier

[63] Except for Mather, Grindall Rawson, pastor at Mendon, was the only member
of the Class of 1678 still alive. Both context and epithet indicate that Rawson, a
noted and frequent preacher to the Indians in their own tongue, was the expected
"Worthy Minister," who, on the second day at Natick, conducted "the Exercises . . .
in the Indian language."

[64] *A True Survey and Report of the Road.* See p. 49 (July 12).

will I be, to do all Good Offices for them. The Less they do to befriend my Prosperity, the more will I Promote their Prosperity, and Rejoice in it. The more they murmur at me in their Tents, the more will I Pray for them in my Study. The more Disaffection they Seem to Express for me, the more Importunity will I use to persuade them, that they would be well-affected unto their Saviour. The Less value they Seem to have for my Ministry, the Richer Entertainments will I Endeavour for them in my Ministry.

27.d 5.m Lords Day.

I Spent this Lords-day, in the Exercises of Religion, with the Garrison at the Castle. I Enjoyed Singular Assistances from the Glorious Lord, in the Services of the Day; and I hope there were precious Impressions Left upon the Auditory.

2.G.D. I must Exceedingly Strengthen the Idea, How Reasonable and Honourable a Thing it is, to make a present of Well-Educated Children unto the Common-Wealth. And more particularly Employ that Thought upon Each of the Children; what shall I do, to render this Child a Blessing to the World? And Cultivate such an Education, of the Child, as may best answer that grand Intention.

This ought frequently to be a Subject of Discourse with my Children, when they Come to an Age Capable of being discoursed withal.

3.G.D. I am afraid, I am afraid, My Wife's Brother hath Sinned away his hopeful Convictions, and Impressions. I must faithfully represent unto him, the danger of his condition.[65]

4.G.D. I am thinking, What if I should Every week, as the News-Letter [66] comes out, Note from it, and also from other Informations that I may have, the Principal Occurrences in this Place;

---

[65] Dr. John Clark. See p. 9, n. 14.

[66] The "Boston News-Letter," America's first regularly published paper, issued its first number on April 28, 1704.

(and some relating to other Places:) and the Dispensations of Divine Providence; Especially on our Indian Troubles. And make a Remark of Piety on Each of them; a Prayer to Heaven on Each of them. This would be a Pious Regard unto the Works of the Lord, and the Operations of His Hands. It is possible also, the Composures may be of great use, at some time or other among the People of God.

5.**G.D.** I would Encourage the Captain of the Castle, to have Something Like a School in the Castle, Where they that have been defectively Educated, may be taught Writing and Cyphering, and Other things that may be profitable for them.

And I would Employ the Hand of the Physician there, to Scatter Books of Piety, and do other Good Offices among them.

6.**G.D.** It may be a Charitable Work, for me to Visit the Young Thieves in the Prison, and Promote the Work of Repentance in them.

7.**G.D.** If it be Possible for me to recover Time and Strength for it, I would more frequently Visit some of the Lectures in my Neighbourhood; not only to Encourage the Labours of my Brethren, but also to make better Improvements in Piety, and usefulness, under such Hints as may occur to me in their Ministrations.

$$\frac{2.d}{3.} \quad 6.m \quad \begin{array}{l} \text{Saturday.} \\ \text{Lords-Day.} \end{array}$$

In this Night I made my Repeated Visit to Heaven, with the Exercises of a *Vigil*.

After Midnight I arose, and Cast myself Prostrate upon the Floor before the Lord, and from thence Cried unto Him, first for the Pardon of my Miscarriages, and then for Such Favours as my Desires were more particularly breathing after. I considered and acknowledged the Holy Spirit as God, and particularly addressed Him as the object of Religious Adoration and Invocation; Hoping that He would please to take the more favourable Notice of me, inasmuch as herein I pay an Homage unto Him, which is denied by so many in the World. I now Entreated the Infinite God, in all His Three Persons, and particularly of the Holy Spirit; that He would Enlighten me in the Knowledge of my admirable Saviour, and give me to know His person, His Natures, and His Beauties; and to display His Glories unto the world. I besought Him to be with me, in an Essay to Conquer Deism, which I am now upon.[67] I besought Him to take a Gracious Care of my Family, and Convert my Children, and Especially to fall upon poor *Increase* with His Converting Influences, and raise up Kind Friends unto them. I besought Him, to Smite One of my Restless and Wicked Enemies with Horror of Conscience, and Restrain him from hurting of me. I Petitioned Him for Good News from a far Country, that may Encourage me and Fortify me in my Serviceableness. I presented my Humble and fervent Petition before Him, that He would Pity my Flock, and forgive all the murmuring in their Tents, and all the Ill Usage, which at any time they treat me withal; And that He would Cure all that is amiss among them, and that He would give a mighty Success to His Word, and prosper my Ministry, and produce a Great Work of Repentance and Conversion in the Neighbourhood, and be with me in the Day which was presently to dawn upon me.

1.**G.D.** Words of a Predictory Strain, which I have let fall in my Sermons, have had a Strange Accomplishment. Hereby a Great Authority is Conciliated unto my Ministry. Some Remarkable Instances have Lately happened. I declared, that I did believe, there were some young Men, whom God would Speedily bring forth, and Leave them to be Tragical Examples of Sin and Misery, and hang them up in Chains for all the Congregation to tremble at; and that I now Lived in a daily Expectation of it. In that very Week, there was a Large Knot of the Wicked Children in this place, detected in a Course of horrid Thieveries and Robberies, and run into prison, and made the Discourse and Wonder of all the Country. There was much Notice taken of this. Again,

---

[67] *Reason Satisfied and Faith Established.* See p. 61 (Aug. 9).

'Tis a Common observation among the People, that if on the Lords-Day, I do with an agreeable Solemnity Let fall Passages of this Importance, that this may be the Last Lords-Day that some of them will have opportunity to be present in the Assemblies of Zion; the Ensuing week is then Signalized with Some very observable Mortality in the Neighbourhood. I have my mind this day under a Strong Impression, to declare my Fears, that there are some of our People, and very particularly Some Young People among us, who are apace Ripening for very Woeful Circumstances. It will not be Long before we see them in very woeful Circumstances. It may be, the Lord will bless this Declaration to do some good among them.

About this time, a Mad Fellow, a Captain of a Ship, (an Utter Stranger to me,) who foolishly imagined, that I intended him, in Some Rebukes that one of my Sermons bestowed upon Vicious Courses; being heated with his Cups at the Tavern, Came to my house about nine o'clock at night, with a drawn Courtelace, and swore Many Oaths, that he would Cleave me down; and said, he would be content to lie a year in Hell, if he might have the Satisfaction of killing me. Some of the Neighbours, Perceiving his Purpose and his Fury, Stopped the Wild beast at my Gate, so that I Saw him not.[68]

2.**G.D.** I ought, whenever I have my Children before me, and there be Time for such a thing, to Entertain them with some Useful Discourse, on some Noble Subject. In this I am not altogether Negligent. But I would improve in my Diligence for their Instruction; And make it a Continual Dropping. And I would Spend some Thoughts, to find out, the most Necessary and agreeable Points of the Paternal Conversation.

3.**G.D.** I would Unite Counsels with my Wife's Eldest Brother,[69] Who is a Justice of Peace; What Good may be done in the Neighbourhood. And being a Physician also, I would in that capacity Study for him, and with him, what good to do.

[68] Mather wrote this passage in the margin opposite the entry for August 2.
[69] Dr. John Clark. See p. 9, n. 14.

$\dfrac{5.\text{d}}{6.}$ 6.m **Tuesday.**
Wednesday.

I found my Spirit under a Strong Impression to Rise an hour after Midnight, and Carry on the Exercises of a *Vigil,* prostrate in the Dust before the Lord. I presented my Various Petitions before the Lord; Such as have of Late been the Occasions for these Exercises. And my desires to be directed about my Son *Increase.* With very particular Supplications, that the Lord would assist me and accept me, to bear a Testimony for His Holy Religion against raging Infidelity.

4.G.D. I am strongly called upon to Compose and Publish a brief Treatise, for the Confutation of *Deism;* Which with ardent Supplications to Heaven, that I may be helped and blessed in my undertaking, I am now Endeavouring.

5.G.D. I hear of an Unhappy knot of young Householders in my Neighbourhood, who misspend much Time together, and Poison and Ruin one another. I would advise with some Good men, about recovering of them.

6.G.D. There is a Child of Poor and Wretched Parents in my Neighbourhood; Which I will Put into the School, and Pay for his Education there.

There is also, a Poor, Aged, Stupid Sinner in my Neighbourhood, not Long for this world; I would make one Essay more, to Save him.

7.G.D. I would be greatly affected with Dispositions of agreeable gratitude unto the Glorious God of my Health, and by the Health with which He favours me, be Awakened unto Such Acknowledgments of Him, and Such Resolutions of Piety, as I think, He more Emphatically Calls me to. Wherefore first; When I Visit the Sick, I would Bless the Lord for my own Freedom from their Diseases; and think, What Moral Diseases and Disorders most analogous to these, I should be watchful against; and unto What Graces and Actions, I should by the Goodness of my Saviour, and first offer my prayers to Him, and then Employ my Cares, for the obtaining of them. There are more particularly Five Grievous Diseases, My Deliverance from which I would improve in a way of Exceeding Thankfulness unto the Lord my Healer. And being so delivered, I would on that Occasion thus Glorify God my Saviour. Since I am not Lying under the Living Death of a *Palsey,* Oh! Let it Engage me to be Very Lively and Active in the Service of God. Since I am not Under the horrible Corrosions of a *Cancer,* Oh! Let all Tendencies to *Envy* be Extinguished in my Soul, with a Perpetual Joy in the Prosperity of my Neighbours. Since the Tortures of the *Gout* are not upon me, Let my Feet Cheerfully carry me, to comfort the Afflicted, and attend the Congregations of the Faithful, and Let my Hands not be Idle in writing for God, and in giving to the poor. Since the *Stone* has not Laid me on the Rock, Let me be full of Tender Compassion to all the Miserable. And Since I am not wasting under a *Consumption,* Let me beware of a Leanness in my Soul; beware of *Pining* away in my Iniquities! This Week, besides my passing through many other Employments, I prepared a Treatise for the press, which was demanded from me,

(VI.) on the occasion of tendencies to Atheistical Theism,[70] discovered in more than I had been aware of. I Entitled it: REASON SATISFIED AND FAITH ESTABLISHED. *The Resurrection of our Glorious JESUS, demonstrated with many Infallible Proofs; and the Holy Religion of a Risen Jesus Victorious over all its Blasphemous Adversaries.*

1.G.D. There is grievous occasion to animadvert, with an Holy Discipline, on Some in the Flock, who Sin against the Covenant of God, under the obligations whereof they have put themselves. I must Endeavour to dispense the most faithful Admonitions on this occasion.

2.G.D. Let me Renew my practice of taking my Capable Children

---

[70] If "Theism" here is not a slip of the pen, Mather is clearly using the term in the early sense of "Belief in the existence of God, with denial of revelation" (*OED*), in accordance with which it is synonymous with *deism.*

Successively, Every Saturday Evening into my Study, and there
Talk to them, and Pray with them, and Settle the Resolutions
of their Souls for Serious Piety.

3.**G.D.** A Sister-in-Law Lately Recovered from Sickness, is a Proper
Subject, for my best Advice, to Glorify Her Saviour, with all
Possible Gratitude and Obedience.

4.**G.D.** In my Letters to *Scotland,* which I am now writing, I will
Sollicit the Gentlemen to Suggest unto me, what Services I may
do for the Interests of God, in that Nation. And I will Particularly animate their Endeavours to Send Missionaries into the
Southern Colonies of *North America.*

13.d 6.m Wednesday.

This Day, the People of *Charlestown* set apart, as a Day of Prayer,
in order to their Calling of another Minister.[71] The Divine Providence ordered it, that I must be the man, upon whom the Principal Services of the Day must be devolved. In the Afternoon, I
prayed and preached, with great Assistances of Heaven; and my
Father Concluded with Prayer.

5.**G.D.** I am thinking, whether I should not Propose unto our Society, to assist the Publication of a Little Book, Suited unto the
Interests of Piety in the Islands of the *Indies,* and Send it thither,
to be Scattered among them, that they may make a Right Use of
the Dreadful Judgments, which God has inflicted on them.[72]

6.**G.D.** There are some Young Persons, Who having passed through
the Services of their Youth, and now Entering into the World,

[71] Finally a minister was selected. On October 13, 1713, the Rev. Joseph Stevens
(H.C. 1703) was ordained colleague of the Rev. Simon Bradstreet (H.C. 1693).
Mather, who in 1698 had extended the "Right Hand of Fellowship" at Bradstreet's
ordination, also participated in this ceremony. See Sewall, II, 401–02 and Mather's
Diary, II, 247. For the various difficulties attending the selection of Bradstreet, see
Mather's *Diary,* I, 226 and 269; and William I. Budington, *History of the First
Church, Charlestown* (Boston, 1845), pp. 111–12. For Mather's estimate of Stevens,
see this volume, pp. 78–79 (Sept. 26).

[72] Presumably this is a reference to the series of violent earthquakes and hurri-
canes that devastated the British West Indies during the summer of 1712.

are out of Employment. I must project and contrive as well as I can, for them.

15.d 6.m Friday.

Though I attended the Duties of a more Public Fast, on the Last Wednesday, yet I now applied myself unto the Duties of a more Private One.

My Occasions and Employments, were the same that I have mentioned for One of my *Vigils,* about a Fortnight ago.

7.G.D. To Rise unto a very Heavenly Temper and Conduct at the Stroke of Sabbatizing, is a thing which I would Endeavour, with a Zeal that shall even Swallow me up. I would therefore Improve in the Methods of Sabbatical Piety; and having invented such by the Wisdom that comes from above, I would take one of the First Opportunities to record after what manner I have Spent my Sabbath; and from thence transfer it into my *Paterna;* that mine also may go and do Likewise.

1.G.D. God has ordered it, that a man of this Neighbourhood has Lately died in very Woeful Circumstances; He has, in a Distemper of Mind seizing on him, horribly Starved himself to Death. I would make use of this Tragical Example, to awaken the Christless ones in the Neighbourhood, and to declare unto them, what a fearful Picture of their own Condition, the Great God has given them in the Woeful Circumstances of this Miserable Man; famishing themselves, and refusing the Food of their Souls. And now they may see, if the Great God arm only their own Souls to Execute His Wrath upon them, there will need no more terrible Executioners. It may be, God will sanctify these warnings, to them.

17.d 6.m Lords Day.

My Endeavour this Day at the Table of the Lord, was to Converse with a Lovely Jesus, as the Food and the Life of my Soul. But finding that I had so Concocted a Glorious Christ into my Soul, that it was become the very Temper of my Soul, to plead His Blood, and Make my Flight unto His Righteousness, and Consider His Holy Example, and Serve His Kingdom and Interest; I had a glorious Assurance raised in me, that He would never Lose His Hold of me, but bring me to be a Beholder of His Glory and a Partaker in it.

2.**G.D.** By Speaking to, and Praying with, my Son *Increase,* I must get Shaped and Settled in his understanding, the true Notion of Living unto God, and Subordinating Every motion and affair of his Life, unto that Grand Intention. Then his Education will proceed in happy Circumstances.

$$\frac{18.d}{19.d} \ 6.m \ \begin{matrix} \text{Monday.} \\ \text{Tuesday.} \end{matrix}$$

I rose in the Midst of the Night, for the Supplications of an Holy *Vigil* before the Lord. Prostrate in the Dust before the Glorious One, I Cried unto Him for Several Favours; Very Particularly, that His Holy Spirit may mightily assist me in the work of displaying to the World, the glories of my Saviour. That He would Cure the Froward Humours in my Flock, and pardon their Follies, and give success to His Word among them. That He would bless my Children, and provide well for them, and give New Hearts to them; and Especially Direct and Prosper the Education of my Son *Increase.* That He would be merciful to One of my personal Enemies, a Very Wicked Man, who lies now Indisposed; and Smite another of them, with a just Horror of Conscience, and Commission his own Soul to do that upon him, that shall Stop him in his Wickedness. But One Very Singular Errand which I went unto Heaven upon, was with Relation to a Certain Woman of some Influence in the world, whom I take to be a very Evil one, and the Cause and Life and Soul of most wretched Circumstances, to those that are under her Influence. I put her into the Hands of the Glorious Lord. I prayed for the Blessings of Goodness to be granted her, and the Turn of her Heart unto Right Things. But, if there were no other way for Blessings to Come at His People, I prayed unto the Lord, that He would Send us Tidings of His having Removed her.

3.**G.D.** I have a Kinsman, who is a Candidate of the Ministry; I would Study ways both to prepare him for Service, and Obtain for him an Improvement in it. [Τοφτε] [73]

4.**G.D.** In my Letters to *Scotland,* and unto St. *Andrews* as well as unto *Glasgow,* I am contriving a Variety of Good Motions to be set forward; needless to be mentioned. But I Particularly write unto the Rector of the School at *Glasgow,* and send him the Book about *Von Extor;* and pray him to have it Read among the Scholars there.[74]

5.**G.D.** Of all the Societies that I belong to, none Seems more to Need an Excitation, to prosecute their Business, than that of the Commissioners for the Indian-affairs. I would Excite them to a greater Frequency in their Meetings, and Earnestly pursue many things for the Evangelical Interests there.

6.**G.D.** There is a Woman in my Neighbourhood, who is Vicious to the Last degree; wallows in all the vices of a Lewd Conversation; grows to an Extreme Height of most notorious Wickedness. There ought to be solemn Admonitions dispensed unto her before the Decree bring forth. I would in the best Ways I can think of, Endeavour the Dispensation.

7.**G.D.** Let the Changes of the Weather be Entertained by me, with Holy Dispositions, and adapted Supplications. When 'tis fair and clear, and the *Sun* Shines out; *Lord, In the Light of thy Sun of Righteousness Let me see Light, and Enjoy a perpetual Serenity!* When the *Clouds* gather, and cover the sky; *Lord, Let*

---

[73] Tofte(?). Forbes suggests that the reference might be to John Tufts (H.C. 1708) whose "mother was Mercy, daughter of the Rev. Seaborn Cotton."

[74] Christlieb Leberecht Von Extor (1697-1707), "Late Son to the Physician of the King of *Prussia*" and a "famous and wondrous Example of EARLY PIETY," is described in Mather's *Man Eating the Food of Angels,* published in 1710. Mather would have been delighted, his soul enravished, if only the interests of his own dear "Cressy" had paralleled those of this exemplary child, the nature of whose tortured being the passages quoted by Holmes (II, 601-02) amply suggest.

not the Face of Heaven be so Clouded and Covered, that my Prayer shall not Pass through! When the *Rain* falls; *Lord, Let the Heavens Rain down Righteousness upon me; and Let my Doctrine distill as the Rain upon my Hearers.*

1.G.D. This Last Week, there has been a Second Instance, following on one a few Months ago, of a wicked and froward Parent wishing the Death of her Child, and the untimely Death of the Child following upon it, (this Last, by Drowning,) I would make this an occasion of dispensing to my Flock, the most Lively Admonitions, concerning the providence of God always at work, and Concerning the Danger of Evil Speeches, and Evil Wishes.

$$\frac{\text{23.d}}{\text{24.d}} \quad \text{6.m} \quad \frac{\text{Saturday.}}{\text{Lords-Day.}}$$

I kept such a *Vigil,* as I did six nights ago. My Occasions and Petitions were the Same, that then Laid me in the Dust before the Lord. Especially the Last of them. After the Devotions were over, I did with some surprise call to mind, that they who by their Memorial before the Throne of God, procured an order for the Hewing down of a Noxious and a Venomous Tree, are called, Dan. IV. 17. *The Watchers and the Holy ones.*[75]

These papers being written for the Instruction of my Children, after I am Dead, as well as for my own Reflection upon them, before I die, I would Serve every Interest of Piety in them, from my own Experience.

I don't Remember, that my *Method of Sabbatizing,* has ever been Particularly described in these Memorials. Wherefore I will now, my Children, describe and recite unto you, how I Spent the Lords-Day, which has now occurred unto me.[76] In the Afternoon

---

[75] Abstraction frequently conceals Mather's readiness to have his particular Agags "hewed in pieces before the Lord."

[76] Mather subsequently implemented his proposal of August 16 (p. 63) by copying this record of "Sabbatical Piety" into the "Paterna" (pp. 290–95) with a few minor changes.

that went before the Lords-Day I was desirous to have my Studies over, and no affairs Left that might be any encumbrance upon me.

And I devoted the Evening to Exercises of Piety.

In the Morning I awoke, Blessing the Lord for another Lords-Day; And I Rose a Little Earlier than on other Days:

I Considered my Usual Question for this Morning, *What Service may I do for the Church to which I am immediately related?*

I Sang my Morning Hymn.

Coming into my Study, I wrote down my answer to my Question.[77]

I applied myself unto the Lord, as for the pardon of my former Trespasses, on the Holy Rest of His Day, through the Blood of Him that is the Lord of it, so for Grace from Him, now to Sanctify this Day, without which I can do nothing.

Throughout all the Ensuing Day, I kept my Thoughts in an agreeable Employment, and under the necessary government. When I was not Engaged in any Extended Exercise of Devotion, I was continually forming Admonitions of Piety, from occasional Objects and Occurrences: Every thing about me Preached unto me; and I usually turned the Lessons into Ejaculatory Prayers. If I found my Mind begin at any time to lie Fallow, and Empty of Good Thoughts, I Presently rebuked it, and renewed them. If any Evil Thoughts began to make the Least approach to my Mind, I presently bewailed it, and rejected them, and raised Good ones just contrary to them.

I So took heed against Sinning with my Tongue, that I did not Utter One Word all the Day, (though I Spoke on many occasions,) but what, I think, I may say, I did well to utter it.

I wrote an Illustration on a Text of the Sacred Scripture.

I read a Suitable Portion of the Old Testament, in the Hebrew Language. Another in the French. And then a Suitable Portion of the New Testament in the Greek. And I fetched a Note and a Prayer out of Every verse.

Then I made the Morning Prayer of my Study.

[77] I.e., he entered his "G.D." for Sunday.

My Breakfast being brought me, my Food was received, with praises to God, and meditations on the nobler provisions, which He has made for my better part. With the Like Frames and Acts, I anon took the other Two Meals of the Day.

I went down to my Family, and Sang and Prayed with them.

I gave new charges unto my Family, to Remember the Sabbath-day, and keep it Holy: And I assigned unto the Little Children, that were to stay at home, Sentences of the Bible, to be got by heart.

I returned unto my Study, and Prayed, that the Public Sacrifices, to which I was now going, might be acceptably and profitably carried on.

I went unto the public, where my Parent performed the public Ministrations.

Here I gave Such Attention, that not One Passage of the Prayer; not one Head, or Text, and Scarce one Sentence in the Sermon, passed, without my Mind moving towards Heaven, with a Suitable Confession or Petition upon it. And Every Verse of the Psalm, I accompanied with a Note and a Wish Educed from it.

When all was finished, I set myself to form the Desires for all the Hearers, and the Desires and Purposes for my own Life, and think on those Improvements in Piety, which the Subject newly handled, might Call me to.

Returning to my Study, I read over some Holy Discourses, relating to the Great Sabbatism, which the Church of God is to Look for; and the Glorious Things that are spoken about the City of God, and the prophecies relating to the Later Days. This I did, (and usually do) because, I Look on the Sabbath, as a Peculiar Type and Sign of the Blessed *Millennium*.

Going to my Table, I fed the Souls of the Company, with as Profitable Discourses as I could Entertain them withal. And I also drew out my Soul to the Hungry. I thought it a day proper to dispense Kindnesses to the poor. I was Careful to have some Such Invited unto my Table.

After this, I went on, upon the affairs of the Great *Sabbatism*.

I read a Paragraph of the Scripture, that refers unto it; with my acutest and most penetrating Thoughts thereupon; and Suitable Ejaculations. And I Sang an Hymn upon it.

Then, Prostrate in the Dust, I poured out a prayer for *Zion in the Dust,* and for the Hastening of the Day of God.

Hereupon I took the Sermon I was to preach immediately, And run it over, so that my mind was formed into Proper Tempers, and Wishes, on every Head of the Sermon.

I then on my Knees, bewailed before the Lord, such Sins, as the Sermon I was to preach, most Led me to Repent of; and prayed for Grace to do such things, as my Sermon was to Exhort my Hearers to; and begged for the Help of Heaven in the work before me.

I went unto the Public, and carried on the Several Services there,[78] in a great Assembly, with a great Assistance from God.

My Mind, between the Conclusion of the Services, and reaching my House, was filled with prayers that what had passed, might make due Impressions on the people.

Excessively tired, I drank my Tea, with praises to my Glorious Lord; and some Thoughts on His Precious Benefits which this Water Led me to.

I made a prayer, such a feeble one as it was, for such Blessings as I am daily to ask for.

I went down unto my Family, where I catechized the Children, and went through the Sermons of the Day with them, in the way of a Dialogue; and Sang and Prayed with them, and with the neighbours that came in, to join with us.

Then I caused the Children to tell me, what new matter of prayer they were now apprehensive of? And Charged them to Retire with it before the Lord.

I also made one of them, to hear the Negro-Servant Say his Catechism.[79]

---

[78] "Paterna" adds the interesting fact that these services consumed "about Three hours" (p. 293).

[79] On December 13, 1706 "Some Gentlemen of [the] Church" presented Mather with "a very likely *Slave,*" whom they had purchased for their minister "at the

I retired unto my Study, and meditated on that point; *What have I yet Left undone, that it would be for my Consolation and Satisfaction to do, before I die?*

I Read in a Book of Piety, a Sermon, that might add unto the Heavenly Tincture on my Mind.

I was Called to pray with a Sick Person; unto which I went with Alacrity, as unto a Duty of the Sabbath.

I went again unto my Family, and Sat with them, while Each of the Capable Children, Successively Read their Several Parts in a Book of Piety, to the whole Family. And I took occasion from thence to Renew my Instructions to them.

Then I sang my Evening Hymn with the Family and retired unto my Study, and in prayer acknowledged the Mercies of the Day past; besought pardon for the Errors of the Day past; Committed all my Interests into the Hands of my dear Saviour; and actually Exerted an Act of a Principle of Grace, that might assure me of my Safety, if I were to die before tomorrow.

So I went unto my Rest, and fell asleep, Reading a Book of Piety.

This Variety of Duty, was all done, with the Help of Heaven, on this Lords-Day. And though it Left me very weary, yet my Spirit now found (and always, Does) those unspeakable Consolations and Advantages from such Indefatigable Sabbatizing, as Carry rich Compensations with them. Yea, in the Conclusion of the Day, I declared before the Lord, that although Some had observed, a Reward of Temporal Blessings in the Ensuing Week, often to Encourage their Sabbatizing, I had now been abounding in the Work of the Lord, without the Encouragement of any such Expectation. If never so much Affliction should befall me this

---

expense of between forty and fifty Pounds." Mather at once named him *Onesimus* and "resolved" to use "the best Endeavours to make him a Servant of Christ" (*Diary*, I, 579). In 1716 Mather granted Onesimus his freedom, apparently more to get rid of him as a trouble-maker than to reward service well rendered: "My Servant *Onesimus*, proves wicked, and grows useless, Froward, Immorigerous. My Disposing of him, and my Supplying of my Family with a better Servant in his Room, require much Caution, much Prayers, much Humiliation" (*Diary*, II, 363).

Week, yet I would go on, in all the Holy Labours of Sabbatizing to Him, and assure myself, that I should find my Account in the Rest that remains for the People of God.[80]

2.G.D. I direct my Daughters to read considerately Mr. *Vincent's* Sermon to Young Women, and give me some Account, what they have met withal.[81]

I will also have my Children provided with Blank Books, whereinto they shall transcribe such passages as have in Reading most affected them. And they shall show me their Books Every Lords-Day Evening.

3.G.D. I would shortly give a Visit unto Each of my Kindred in *Charlestown,* and therein discourse unto them Such things as may be for their advantage.[82]

4.G.D. I know not why I may not Enter among my projections of Services, the Journey which I have this day before me. Whenever I travel abroad, it Leaves Precious Impressions on the places where I Come, and the Lord Strangely Smiles upon my going out and my coming in. It may Considerably serve the Kingdom of God, for me now and then to go abroad.

27.d 6.m Wednesday.

I rose in the Middle of the Night, and made a short supplication, for a Blessing on the Service of the Day Ensuing. (And also relating to the Last Article of the Vigils Lately Mentioned: which is, I believe, obtained.) In the Morning I Went unto *Dedham,* and Enjoyed a mighty Assistance from Heaven, in the Lecture which I preached there. I returned home in the Evening, and finished a Journey full of Comfortable Circumstances.

[80] At this point, and clearly at a time later than that of the original transcription, Mather adds to "Paterna" (p. 295): "But [I] renounced all pretence to *merit* in my own Performances."

[81] Possibly a reference to Thomas Vincent (1634–1678), *Christ the Best Husband: or, An Invitation of Young Women unto Christ* (London, 1672).

[82] Possibly the family of Colonel John Phillips of Charlestown, whose daughter Abigail (1670–1702) had been Mather's first wife.

I Chose to take in the Chariot with me, a Knight of my Acquaintance; and Employ all the most Exquisite Artifice of Insinuating Address, that I may gain him over to serious Piety. I think, my Discourses made, through the Blessing of God, a great Impression on him.

5.**G.D.** Some further provision for the Restraint of Children that play on the Lords-Days, and particularly in the Time of the Public Service; must be promoted.

6.**G.D.** There are Young Men come from other Countries, now residing among us. Their Friends beyond-Sea, will be greatly comforted if they hear well of them, greatly obliged if any good be done for them. I would single out Some such persons for my Special Counsels and Kindnesses.

7.**G.D.** When I am called out of my Study, to speak with any one in my Parlour, I would have Such Wishes as these going up to Heaven, as I am going down to them. *Lord, prepare me for, and assist me in whatever Service may be now before me. And if I am going to Encounter any Sorrow, Let me be prepared for that also!*

1.**G.D.** Having finished my Course of Sermons on the Parable of the *Tares*,[83] I would employ a few Sermons, that may directly subserve to all the Intentions of the Word of God, upon the Minds of the Flock. If the Lord will assist me to handle wisely, the *Seventh, Eighth,* and *Ninth* Verses in the XIX Psalm, I may Come at the whole Flock, in all the points wherein their Edification is to be Endeavoured. My God, I ask thy Assistances!

2.**G.D.** I will have my Son *Increase,* to Study the Greek, *Regulae Vitae,* in *Posselius.*[84] And also to turn them into Latin Verse. And I will Endeavour to Inculcate those Maxims of Piety upon him; and oblige him, what I can, to Practice them.

---

[83] "I preached on Matth. 13.24. The Church on Earth, being the *Kingdom of Heaven* upon Earth. And began my Course of Sermons on the Parable of the Tares" (entry for March 3, 1711/12, "The Course of My Public Ministry," *Diary,* II, 168). For the conclusion of this sermon sequence, see the entry for 31.d 6.m on p. 131 of this present volume.

[84] Johann Posselius the "elder" (1528–1591)?

3.G.D. It must now be more than ever (if that be possible,) my Study to render the Life of my Aged Father Easy. I Will every day Visit him, with particular Contrivances for his Ease, his Peace, his Joy, and his Comfortable Fruitfulness.

4.G.D. I propose this Week, if the Glorious Lord will grant it, a Journey to *Salem*. And as I would there do Good in as Many Ways as I can devise, I would Particularly Prepare, if I have Time, a Sermon for the People there, on Psal. LXXVI. 2. *His Tabernacle in Salem;* and Show *Salem* the Methods of obtaining the Happiness, that the Glorious Lord may have His Tabernacle there.[85]

5.G.D. I May do well, to write unto Mr. *Jameson,* the Professor of History, in the University of *Glasgow,* to undertake the History of the Judgment of the Ante-nicene Fathers, concerning the Eternal Deity of Our Saviour. Though he were blind from his Infancy, yet he has a most Prodigious Insight into Antiquity. And for a Blind Man to Confute the Presumptuous *Arians* of this Age, will be a most Illustrious Triumph of Truth over its Adversaries.[86]

6.G.D. I am going this Day to *Salem;* Thither would I Carry Bibles, and Other Books of Piety to be dispersed among the Poor; and if I find any very singular objects of Compassion (which I will Enquire after,) I will do what I can, for them.

5.d 7.m Friday.

I went unto *Salem,* and Enjoyed a manifold Smile of Heaven upon me in my Journey; Accompanied with Two kind Gentlemen of my Neighbourhood, as well as with two of my own children.

7.G.D. I find, that though the Tolls of the Bells for Funerals, do

---

[85] *A Town In Its Truest Glory.* See p. 79 (Sept. 28).

[86] "William Jameson (*fl.* 1689–1720) lecturer on history . . . and presbyterian controversialist" (*DNB*, X, 672).

The University of Glasgow had conferred on Mather the degree of Doctor of Divinity late in 1710. During the remainder of his life he was gratefully appreciative of the honor.

use to raise in me Thoughts and Prayers relating to my own Mortality, yet they have not been so Lively as they ought to have been. I would therefore improve, and grow more Vigorous, in this Exercise of Piety.

1.**G.D.** It may be of use to me, in the service of God, and of Souls very much to Endear myself unto the Children of my Flock, Their Affection to me, may prepare them for Benefit by me. I would therefore invent and Employ the most Winning ways, of Engaging them unto me.

7.d 7.m Lords Day.

I Enjoyed a Mighty Presence of the Glorious Lord with me, at *Salem;* Where I Preached both parts of the Day, such things, as I hope, have Left a deep and Long Impression on the Auditory. I there also Enjoyed the Communion at the Table of the Lord.

2.**G.D.** The Children which I have with me, in my Calash to and from *Salem,* will in the Journey have opportunities for Several Instructions from me.

3.**G.D.** But then, the Children of the Family where I Lodge must be, for the Time, Looked on, as my own Children or as if Related unto me. I do therefore bestow Bibles, and Other Books of Piety among them, and Engage them with presents, to the Love of Piety.

9.d 3.m Tuesday.

I returned home; and neither I nor the Gentlemen with me, were able to mention, so much as One Disagreeable or Inconvenient Circumstance that had befallen us, in all our Journey. It was filled with the Mercies of the Lord.

4.**G.D.** There are several Places, wherein things are out of Order; and my assistance particularly to bring forward the Good Settlement of a Minister, will be of use unto them. I would Endeavour to afford them, in the best manner I can; Particularly, *Salem* and *Charlestown*.

5.G.D. I would quicken some Gentlemen, who have acquainted themselves with the *American* plants, to Communicate what they know thereof, that so there may be accession made unto the general Stock of knowledge, and Botanology particularly Cultivated in the World, and more done to relieve the Miseries of Mankind.

6.G.D. Some in this place, are at this time, Lying Sick in very rueful Circumstances, of Poverty. I must myself Relieve them, and procure also Reliefs from others for them.

7.G.D. By the Disingenuous Carriage of my Unworthy and Ungrateful People towards me, I would be So far from Overcome into a defective Carriage towards them, that I would Maintain the perfect Reverse of it. I would Speak favourably and respectfully of them. I would give the Most Friendly Visits unto them. I would Relieve all their poor. I would most heartily rejoice in all Points of Prosperity, wherewith God smiles upon any of them. I would not fail in any part of the Pastoral Duty, but abound in the work of the Lord.

I had forgotten to insert, that on 12.d 7.m Friday, I Set apart the Day, for Supplications, on the usual Occasions; and Especially that I may be prepared for (if it may be, Comfortable) Tidings from *England*. But my Performances this way, are so poor and mean, that they deserve indeed forever to be forgotten.

1.G.D. What I resolved yesterday, Suits well enough with the Subject assigned for this Day. But I will add, I must fetch another Public Stroke, at that Grand Bond of Iniquity, Evil Company, wherein so many of our Children are Entangled; and do it with all the solemnity of an Entire Discourse upon it.

14.d 7.m Lords Day.

At the Table of the Lord, I Considered the Blessed JESUS, First, as my High-Priest; and then, as my Prophet, and my King. I received Him, I embraced Him, I adored Him, in all of those Glorious Offices. I declared before Him, the precious Things which I depended on Him, to do for me in them all.

2.G.D. I would afford more Time unto my Children and Family, in the Latter Part of the Evenings; and Employ it in Conferences with them, on the most noble and useful Subjects. Very particularly, I would go through a *Cosmology,* in my Conferences with them.

3.G.D. I have a Kinsman in my Next Neighbourhood, of whom I ought to take a Renewed and Special Notice, with Admonitions of Piety; And I will Endeavour to do so accordingly.

4.G.D. Would it not serve the Interests of Piety, very particularly in the Town of *Salem,* and also in other places, to which I may Send it, if I should Publish my Late Sermon at *Salem;* directing the Methods of becoming an happy Town?

5.G.D. I am writing to a very Capable, but a very Covetous, Person at *Salem;* to Stir him up unto Some Expenses of his Revenues, on Pious Uses. And particularly, for the dispersing of Certain Books of Piety, which his own Town has particular occasion for.

The Ministers of this Town have disbursed Liberally towards a New Edition of the *Letter of the aged N.C. Ministers,*[87] that we may disperse it through the Country; Especially where People are most in danger of being drawn into an Apostasy to the Superstitions of the Ch. of E. I will prevail with our Society, to advance a Little money, for the forwarding of the same Intention.

6.G.D. There is a Family of our Church fallen into very great Poverty, by the Long sickness of the Poor woman in it. I will afford them some Relief; and procure more for them. [Ρεινολδς] [88]

---

[87] *A Letter From Some Aged Nonconforming Ministers . . . Touching the Reasons of their Practice* (Holmes, *Increase Mather, a Bibliography,* No. 144) had already appeared in London printings of 1701, 1702, and 1704. A Boston edition with a four-page "To the Reader" signed by Increase Mather and dated "August 8th" appeared in 1712.

[88] Reynolds.

7.G.D. Many Thoughts I have had, about the Nature and the Design of *Laughter; that* odd Action, *Laughter.* If it be nicely and narrowly Examined, it seems to be Little Other, than a Sudden Triumph of Pride, upon our Perceiving of Others to be in Circumstances inferiour to our own; but most of all, upon a Quick Apprehension, that the Follies of Others, are such as we are not ourselves Guilty of. More than Seven Efforts of Laughter in Ten, really are no other than the Operations of a proud Conceit we have of ourselves. Behold, A Refined Essay of the Christian *Asceticks!* First I must by no means make myself a part of any Company, who make it their Business to Laugh. And then, as I would be slow to Laugh, so upon provocations to it, I would accurately Enquire, *would not an humble Charity bespeak a Pity for this object, rather than a Laughter?* and govern myself accordingly. All proud Satisfactions in my own Superiorities, must be Mortified in me, and Extinguished. I must be Watchful against all ebullitions of pleasure in opportunities to Cast Contempt upon Other People. And those which discover themselves in Laughter, are particularly to be watched over. And, if in the issue, I find myself confined unto a Perpetual Seriousness, where is the Damage of it? Never do we read of our Great Saviour, that at any time *He Laughed.*

1.G.D. I may do well, to repeat a Charge upon my Flock, with a more than ordinary and an ungainsayable Importunity, that they betimes inform their Children, What they were *Baptized* for? I would also myself do it, both in my Sermons, and in my Catechizing. And I would in the Baptismal Prayers mightily prosecute the Same Intention. The Benefits of abounding more than we do (though I have done much this way,) in this method of Piety, will be unspeakable. But I am suspicious, that shortly there may be Temptations to the growth of Anabaptism in my Neighbourhood. And Piety Operating this way, will be a special Antidote.

2.G.D. My Little Son *Samuel,* mightily improves in Reading, and gives his Mind unto it. I would on this happy Occasion Exceedingly Encourage him: And set him things to Read and Learn; and Reward him, when he has done.

3.**G.D.** The gentlewoman, who is the Widow of my Kinsman once at *Hampton,* being removed unto *Brookline,*[89] I would Concern myself to do as many good Offices for her, and hers, as I can; and for her only Son particularly. I have one at this time in View.

I have a Kinsman also, a School-master at *Beverly,* to whom I would give certain Books that may be useful for him; and my best Counsels.[90]

4.**G.D.** There are Several Services to be done for the Cause of Christianity among the Indians; Particularly, a Large Tract of Land, may be procured for them near *Dartmouth,* where we may settle a pretty Village of them in Christian Circumstances. I would form an Address to our General Assembly upon it, and get our Commissioners to Engage in it.

5.**G.D.** The People of the old Church, hold a Monthly Lecture, in this time of their Dispersion;[91] and at it they have a Collection, for the Support of their Ministers, in some of their Domestic Expenses. I would not only give my own Presence at it, but also Encourage Many Others to visit it, and Contribute on that Occasion!

6.**G.D.** At *Charlestown* they have Chosen a Minister, who has a bad Reputation for Levity, and Vanity, yea, and for disaffection to good Men and Things.[92] I must use a Method, that this

---

[89] Mrs. Ann (Lake) Cotton. See "3.G.D." and p. 34, n. 40.

[90] John Cotton (H.C. 1710), later to become minister at Newton, "began to teach school at Beverly . . . shortly after commencing B.A." Mr. Shipton adds (Sibley, V, 517) that Cotton "moved among the Essex County aristocracy, and whenever he went to Boston he stayed with his famous relative, Cotton Mather." See p. 85, n. 95.

[91] The building of the First Church had been destroyed in the fire of 1711 and was not replaced until 1713.

[92] The Rev. Joseph Stevens. See p. 62 and n. 71. I can find nothing whatever to substantiate Mather's charges. Forbes suggests plausibly that it was, perhaps,

Person be well advised of the Just Expectation which both God and Men have concerning him.

7.G.D. I feel an Unknown Illness hanging about me. It Looks Like a Tendency to a Fever. I know not what will be the Progress and Issue of it. I would this Day Spend some time Extraordinary in those Prayers, and other Cares, that may be necessary for the Dispatch of every thing, that may render my Death Comfortable to me, if I Must now be called unto it.

1.G.D. There is a Woman of uncommon Accomplishments, in this Neighbourhood, who if she were Effectually drawn to Serious Piety, and joined unto the People of God, would prove a great Blessing to our Church. I will use a variety of the most Exquisite methods I can devise, to accomplish it.

About this Time, I fitted for the Press, the discourse I Lately delivered at *Salem*. I furnished it with some Additional Inculcations of Holy Sabbatizing, and Preservatives from the Contagion of Quakerism, which I thought might Singularly serve the Interests of Religion, in that, as well as in some other Towns. My purpose is, to present many Scores of this Book, unto the Families of *Salem;* and some Scores to some other Towns. I therefore give it unto the Bookseller; under this Title.

A TOWN IN ITS TRUEST GLORY: *A Brief Essay upon, A Town happy and glorious. Recommending those things by which a Town may come to flourish with all Prosperity. A Discourse wherein the State of all our Towns is Considered; But the Peculiar Temptations and Occasions of Some Towns among us, are more particularly accommodated.*

VII.)

2.G.D. One Precious Way of my Redeeming the Time, with and for my Children, will be, Often when I am Sitting with them, to Single out some Article of Religion, and ask them, How they will prove it; Show them, how to prove it; And pro-

---

Stevens's "connection at this time with Harvard as Tutor and Fellow of the Corporation that gave Mather this opinion of him." See Budington, *History of the First Church, Charlestown.*

ceed then, to discourse on the Holy use, that must be made of it.

My Conversation with my son *Increase,* may now be so managed, as to sharpen both of us, for the ready and fluent Speaking of Latin.

3.**G.D.** I have a Brother-in-Law, in whom I wish I could see a brighter Shine of Piety, and a better Effect of the Awakenings he has met withal. Fresh Losses, and hard ones, are inflicted on him, in his Interests at Sea. I would use the best means I can, that the Dispensations of God may be Sanctified unto him.

4.**G.D.** I would Send unto the Southern Colonies, where they may Extremely want them, some Numbers of the Book we have lately Published, *The Letter of the aged N.C.s* that so the People of God, there, may be fortified against their Enemies; and Established in the Present Truth.

5.**G.D.** Methinks, it should not be amiss for me, My Lecture falling this year, on the Second of *October,* the memorable Day of the burning of the Town, to make it an opportunity of delivering such things as I have prepared in my Discourse of, *A Town in its truest Glory!*

6.**G.D.** There is a gentleman, who has been formerly very Abusive to me, but remarkably Repents of it. He is now in danger of being Led away with grievous Distempers, and Temptations. I will study all the most Exquisite ways I can, to rescue him.

7.**G.D.** In reading the *European* Papers of Intelligence I am Continually Entertained with Passages, wherein, the Ignorance, the Wickedness, and the Misery of Mankind is discovered. As these passages occur to me, I would make them occasions, to Exercise the Suitable Dispositions of Piety. Some of them will be Expressed in Such Applications of my mind unto the glorious Lord. *Lord, I adore thy Sovereign Grace, in that thou hast not Left me to such miserable Circumstances! And, Lord, what woeful Effects has the Fall and Sin of Man brought upon the World! And, Lord, Pity these poor people, and bring them into a better*

Condition! And, *O my great Saviour, Do thou hasten thy Return, and Rescue Mankind from the Curse that is upon it!*

1.G.D. It may be for the Welfare of the Church, to have it furnished with a Sufficient Committee, of Gentlemen, who may have at heart the Temporal Affairs of the Church, and be ready on all occasions to advise and order, such things as may be for common benefit.

2.G.D. I Will Encourage my Wife, not only to oblige the Neighbours, by giving frequent Visits unto them, but also to observe that Rule in her Visits; to Contrive Some Good in them, and be able to say, when she comes away, that Some Good has been done, where she was.

3.G.D. There are Some Exceeding Remotely akin to me, but Yet such as Value themselves upon claiming a Kindred unto me. I Would recollect, who these are, and Study to dispense Benefits to every one of them. Very Particularly, to one Family in my Neighbourhood; in which there is a young Man, that My Advice may be of use unto.

4.G.D. Inasmuch as the Glorious Lord, has wondrously taken off the Fetters, that were once upon my Speech, and Employed me, though I were once a great Stammerer, in more Speeches, and on greater Occasions, than any man in the Land, I Owe something Extraordinary by way of gratitude, unto Him who has done this wonderful Thing. I have often thought, that it would be worth the while, for me to Write a Little Book for *Stammerers;* directing them, What Holy Improvement they shall make of their Infirmity, and how they shall behave themselves under it. They are a Numerous Generation, in the World.

5.G.D. Though my Relation to our College, be a very Imperfect Sort of a Thing, Yet I would Look on that, in Conjunction with other Considerations, as Obliging me to do all I can for the Welfare of it. Among Other Thoughts this way, I now think, that I will Cultivate an Acquaintance, with the Principal Scholars, and by their means, fill the College with such Books as may

Convey much of the Salt of Truth and Piety, among the Students there.

6.G.D. There is a poor Woman of our Church, who has a very Wicked Husband; and by Sickness to which his Wicked Carriage has Contributed, her Condition is indeed full of Poverty and Misery. I will take all due Care for the Relief of this object. [Φοξ] [93]

7.G.D. The Sweet Mystery of Going to God as my *Father,* and crying, *Abba, Father,* I would Penetrate further into it, than ever I have done; and put it into practice, with the most Lively Strains of the most Evangelical Piety: and then Commend it unto the people of God.

11.d 7.m Saturday.

This Day I Endeavoured it. I Set apart this Day, for Prayer with Fasting, in Secret, before the Lord. I have Thoughts of Changing my Times, from Fridays to Saturdays, for these purposes. I did this Day, though the Chief of Sinners, go to the Great God, as to my Father; Encouraged by the Relation, which my Lovely Jesus bears unto Him; and my Assurance, that the Choice and Wish of my Soul, is to be found among the People of the Blessed Jesus. The Occasions and Petitions for this Day, were such as were usual with me; relating to my Ministry, and my Family, and the Distressed Condition of the People of God, at home and abroad. But One very Particular Intention was, to prepare for whatever Tidings may be coming to me, from the other side of the Water; that I might Submit Patiently and Cheerfully, to whatever Disappointments and Humiliations may be ordered (if any such be ordered) for me; and glorify the Justice, and Wisdom, and Faithfulness of the Lord in them all; that yet, I may have such things arrive unto me, as may Encourage me in the Service of the Lord; and fortify me in my poor Essays to do good in the world.

1.G.D. Intending this Week, if the Lord Please, a Meeting for

[93] Fox.

the Brethren of the Church, I would make it an opportunity, to Speak such things, as may Sweeten their Affections to One another, and beget a due Temper in them; and make them sensible of the Duty they owe unto the Lord, and unto one another.

12.d 8.m Lords Day.

My Principal Endeavour at the Table of the Lord, was, to Express the Spirit of Adoption, in the *Abba, Father,* of Christianity, and in Considerations of the Great God as our Father, and Love and Praise the Glorious JESUS, who brings His people into such a Dignity.

2.G.D. Having allowed unto my Servant *Onesimus,* the conveniences of the Married State, and great Opportunities to get money for himself, I would from hence take occasion mightily to inculcate on him, his obligations to keep the Rules of Piety, and Honesty; and Particularly Charge him, to devote Part of his gains to Pious Uses.

3.G.D. That my Father may be made Easy in his Old Age, I would assist a Wise and Kind Conduct of the Church towards him; that he may Preach as often as he Please; and as often as he finds it may be irksome, command What Help he Please; and all Possible Encouragements from the Church, be Continued unto him, and unto his Family.

4.G.D. I Propose to do some Good, at *Woburn,* and the Neighbour towns, by giving the People, a Lecture there. Which this Day, 15.d 8.m I Endeavoured. And the Lord Graciously Smiled upon me, in my Journey and my Service.

5.G.D. Certain People neglect the Public Worship of God; I would this Evening procure our Society, to take Notice of them, and of some Other Offenders. And in the Society, as also unto the Ministers, I would communicate such a View of the awful Prospect of things at this Day, as may quicken our Supplications.

6.G.D. I would Endeavour a generous present unto our Worthy Friend, Mr. *McNish,* on Long Island; who has met with Difficulties and Discouragements and also been at some Expenses for the Public Service.[94]

7.G.D. There is a dismal Prospect before us. And God knows, what share this poor Country may have, in the Calamities, which threaten to overwhelm a Wicked world. God calls me to more than ordinary Methods, that I may be hidden in the Day of these Calamities; and assist His People also, to get into their Hiding-places. I would therefore make this, more than ever, an Article of Importunate Supplications. And Study and Follow those other methods of Piety, which have the Promise of Preservation annexed unto them.

1.G.D. Having my Catalogue of the Communicants in my Flock; I would sometimes go over it, and in doing so, I would think, What may be the Special Points of Christianity, which Each Person may need Most of all to be advised of. And when I have Opportunity, I would most insist on those Points in my Conversation with them.

[94] George McNish, a Scotchman who came to this country in 1705, served as minister of the Presbyterian Church in Jamaica from 1711 until his death in 1723. Mather's *Diary* entry for November 21, 1711 suggests his part in the arrangement. "The Town of *Jamaica,* on *Long Island,* is a sort of a Frontier for the Interests of the Nonconformists and of true Piety in these Colonies. The Settlement of a worthy Minister there, would be a real Service to Religion. I have already laboured pretty far in it, and brought it near to an Accomplishment. But some further Strokes are necessary, which I [am] now endeavouring to give that it may be perfectly accomplished" (II, 132).

Sprague's *Annals of the American Pulpit* (III, 13–14) contains an interesting commentary on relations between conformist and nonconformist churches in Colonial America: "During the whole of Mr. McNish's ministry, there was a violent controversy carried on in reference to the place of worship in Jamaica, which, though originally built for the Presbyterian Church, was appropriated, by Lord Cornbury, to the use of the Church of England. Though Mr. McNish was the minister of the congregation, some ten or eleven years, it is supposed that he never preached in the house of worship belonging to it, after his installation, as it was not restored till some time after his death."

19.d 8.m Lords Day.

This Day, besides the Other Devotions of the Day, I did in my Study, Pray for Every One of my Church, (near four hundred persons) Each of them Distinctly, by Name, and besought the most Suitable Blessings, that I could think of asking Heaven to bestow upon them.

2.G.D. Whenever I give any thing to my Children, upon their Desire, or without it, be it Money, or any thing Else that may be grateful to them, I would always Let fall a Maxim of Piety, and signify to them, that if they Will Believe and Practice that Maxim, it will be of much more worth and use unto them, than that Little Thing which I now bestow upon them.

3.G.D. I am Still upon the Design of doing more than ever to make my Father's Last Months Comfortable to him. I Will See him Every day, and forever Study Something or other in Every Visit, that may Carry in it some Refreshment unto him, and Something also that may be of an heavenly Tendency.

21.d 8.m Tuesday.

This Day was Kept with the People of *Newtown*, as a Day of Prayer, to obtain the Conduct and Blessing of God, in their Choice of a New Minister. I had a very Comfortable Journey out and home, and Enjoyed a mighty presence of the glorious Lord with me, in the Services of the Day, almost all of which, were imposed on me to be performed.[95]

[95] Typically, Sewall records the event with greater specificity if less rapture: "8r. 21. Dr. Mather, Mr. Walter, I and my Son Joseph ride in the Coach to Newton, to assist in keeping a Fast there, to Pray GOD's Direction of them in Calling a Minister. Mr. Walter prays, Dr. C. Mather Preaches and Prays. Sup with Mr. Hobart's Daughter. *Laus Deo*" (II, 364). Elsewhere Sewall touchingly suggests his sense of private loss: "Mr. Nehemiah Hobart, a very worthy Minister of Newton about 8 miles from hence, died the 25th of August last, in the 64th year of his Age. He is much lamented. I have a particular loss; in that he was a very good Old Friend"

4.G.D. There are Some Churches, much out of order; for whose welfare, I must, as I have opportunity Concern myself. Especially that at *Woodbridge,* from which I am cried unto.[96]

5.G.D. The Ministers of this Town, shall join with me in Writing a Letter, as well as making a Present, unto Mr. *McNish,* to hearten him.

6.G.D. There is a Good, and a very Poor, woman of *Cambridge,* who often Visits my Family, and Encounters with Difficulties and Necessities. I will dispense Reliefs unto her. [Κοοκ][97]

7.G.D. *Purity, Purity,* is that unto which I am under the greatest obligations. I will this Day Study a Description of Holy *Purity,* and with Unutterable Groans Press after a Conformity to it. I gave it in a Sermon, on Psal. 19. 8. to which I refer.

1.G.D. The Time of year is Coming on, wherein the poor of the Flock will need our more than Ordinary Care and Charity, that they may be provided for. I would Endeavour both Publicly and Privately, to blow up the Flame.

2.G.D. My Maid-Servant must be Earnestly called upon, to give all Diligence, that she make her Calling and Election sure. With my Admonitions I will Put a Proper Book into her hands.

3.G.D. I will Study what may be my mother's peculiar Temptations, Exercises, Disadvantages; and with proper Discourses Endeavour to Edify her, and fortify her, against them.

4.G.D. I am advised of a Combination among the People of God, in *England,* for to Set apart One Hour Extraordinary Every Week, that they may Each one in his Closet, Cry to God, for His Appearing to deliver his Church, from the Dangers now threatening of it.[98] I would Set forward a Motion of this Nature among the People of God, in this Country. It may be attended with wondrous Consequences.

(*Letter-Book,* I, 13). Hobart (H.C. 1667) had been Newton's pastor for more than forty years. He was not replaced until November 1714, when John Cotton (H.C. 1710) became minister there.

[96] Cf. p. 31, n. 39.   [97] Cook.

[98] This is Mather's first mention of the proposal fully set forth in the anonymous printed letter which is stitched between the entries for January 27 and 28; see p. 101 and pp. 101 and 113, nn. 19 and 32.

5.G.D. And Particularly would I recommend and prosecute this proposal, in our Societies.

6.G.D. There are two persons in our Church, who have been in great Reputation for Piety; but have abandoned themselves unto a fond, and at best, a very indiscreet Conversation with Each other, on which there has Ensued a grievous Discourse in the Neighbourhood. I must use my best Methods to retrieve what is amiss.

7.G.D. Besides what I do in my Other Supplications, I have thoughts of Setting apart an Hour Extraordinary, about Eight o'clock, Every Tuesday Morning, to represent before the Lord, the condition of His Church at this Day in the world, and Sollicit for His Appearance to do wonderful things, to rescue His People out of their Threatening Circumstances. By such an Exercise, I shall not only prove myself a Living Member in the Body of our Saviour; but I shall befriend all the Intentions of Piety in my Heart and Life. It must needs Leave a Savoury Impression on my Spirit; and it will also Qualify me the More for the public prayers, wherein I am to go before the People of God.

1.G.D. My Catechizing-Exercise, will furnish me, with notable Opportunities, to instill Documents of Piety, into the Minds of the Rising Generation. I would mightily Consider, what may be most Necessary and Seasonable. At this time, I will Particularly fortify the Children against the Superstitions of the Ch. of E. whereto Temptations are Likely to multiply among us.

2.G.D. It is time for me to initiate my Son *Increase,* in the Methods of usefulness. I will show him the Methods, how to *Do Good* Every Day; and in my Conversation with him in the Evening, I will often Enquire of him, What Good he has done.

3.G.D. I would Engage my Brother-in-Law, the Minister of *Roxbury,*[99] in several Holy Designs; but very Particularly to prose-

---

[99] The Rev. Nehemiah Walter (H.C. 1684), minister at Roxbury from 1688 till 1750, married Mather's sister Sarah. Their son Thomas (H.C. 1713) settled at Roxbury as his father's colleague in 1718. They received frequent mention in Mather's published *Diary.*

cute among the more Pious people of his Flock, the purpose of Extraordinary prayers, Every Tuesday Morning; Which this Morning I do myself make a Beginning upon.

4.**G.D.** My Book of, *A Town in its Truest Glory,* being now Published, I would make a present of a Great Number of them, unto the Town of *Salem,* with a Letter unto Some of their principal persons relating to the Dispersion of them. And I would Send them into other Towns, with *To be Lent,* written on them.

5.**G.D.** The Consideration of the Poor, for the Approaching Winter, must particularly be Commended unto the Societies. And the Method of drawing the Good People of the Country, into the Combination for an Hour of Prayer. Whether to publish a Letter, which I may write concerning it.

6.**G.D.** In my Catechizing Exercise (at which this Week, I had near One hundred and fifty Lads,) I would find out, what Lad is able to Read, But so poor that his parents cannot well furnish him; and I would bestow Still a Bible (One at a time,) on such a Child.

7.**G.D.** There is an Error in my Conversation. I allow too much of my Evening Time, unto the Visits of my Neighbours. The Time would be more fruitfully Spent in my Study: Particularly, in transferring into my *Quotidiana,* from *The Works of The Learned,* and from the *Philosophical Transactions,* and from the German *Ephemerides,*[1] and other things, those Treasures which may furnish and Enrich me, for my many Services. I would accordingly Endeavour, a Reformation of this Error; and be more Sparing in my Visits, than formerly.

8.d 9.m Saturday.

This Day I Set apart for Prayers and Alms, with Fasting, on such occasions, as heretofore. Nothing Extraordinary occurred in the Day.

[1] The German counterpart, begun in 1670, to the *Philosophical Transactions* of The Royal Society of London. The complete title is "Miscellanea Curiosa Medico-Physica Academiae Naturae Curiosorum, *sive* Ephemeridum Medico-Physicarum Germanicarum *Curiosarum.*"

1.G.D. My God, Show me, Show me, what Subject I shall in my Ministry next proceed upon. I cry to thee, for thy Direction and Assistance, in fulfilling of my Ministry.

9.d 9.m Lords Day.

This Day, at the Table of the Lord, I pursued Especially Two Intentions. First, I considered the glorious Priesthood of my Saviour, and I made choice of Him, as the Priest, by whom I hope to be Reconciled unto God, and I Exercised Faith on Him, as both my Sacrifice, and my Advocate. Secondly, I made my Application unto my Saviour, for the Communication of the Grace, which the peculiar Circumstances of this Dark Day do call for; The Grace, to know my own Work in this Day, the Testimonies I am to bear for My Glorious Lord; [I am willing and Ready for them; Here I am; O my Lord, Send me!] and the work which the Lord Himself is going to do; and the Grace to bear with Wisdom, Courage, and Patience, all the Trials, to which I may be in this day Exposed.

2.G.D. My Little Son *Samuel,* now grows ready at such Performances; and therefore I will Supply him Continually with Distichs, both Latin and English, to be Learned by Heart, and Rewards upon his Learning of them: and at the Same time Still inculcate this, that his Learning Enriches him far more than the Rewards.

3.G.D. The Governor of Connecticut is akin to me; He is also going to Marry a Gentlewoman who is near akin to me.[2] I would improve my opportunities in Conversation with him, to project, and suggest, many Services to be done, for the advancing of knowledge and goodness in the world, and particularly in the Colony that is under his Government.

4.G.D. I would more than ever promote this Intention among

---

[2] Gurdon Saltonstall (H.C. 1684), minister of New London, served as Governor of Connecticut from 1707 until 1724. His sister was the wife of Mather's relative, the Rev. Mr. Roland Cotton. In November 1712, Gov. Saltonstall married Mrs. Mary Clark, daughter of William and Mary Whittingham, and widow of William Clark of Boston.

our more Superiour People, that they Shall bring this Point of
Conversation, more into fashion, that when they have their
Interviews, they shall not part, until they have Considered,
What Good may be done; and What Good Fruit there may be
of their having been together. My own Circumstances are grown
such, as to render me, more able to Command all Conversation
where I come than I was, while a younger man.

5.G.D. The State of the Indian Churches on the Island of *Nantucket,* Calls for more than ordinary Care concerning them. I
would, as Soon as the Season for it will allow, procure a Council
of Neighbour-Churches, to Visit them, and with Authority, and
according to their best Discretion, Order and Settle things
among them.[3]

6.G.D. There is a very Poor Family, or two, a Little to the North-
ward of me, to be Looked after. [Βαρνς & Ελδριδγε] [4] And a poor
Minister in the Country, whose wants I am to do Something
for. [Μετκαλφ] [5]

7.G.D. The Lord Calls me, to Express in the Daily Devotions
of my Family, a Concern for the Condition of His People in
the World, now a more than ordinary Distress is Come upon
them. I would therefore add these Petitions, to my Daily Sacrifices.

*O Purify and Multiply thy People, and Let those that are
Suffering for thee, be wondrously Supported and Relieved in
their Sufferings. Let all the Plots in the Head of the Old Serpent,
against thy People and Interest be gloriously defeated. Appear*

[3] Mather reports in 1710 (*Bonifacius,* p. 195) that among the Indians "at *Nantucket,* there are at least Three Congregations: and more than as many Preachers."
In his *History of Nantucket* (Boston, 1835) Obed Macy states that the Indians "at
one time had four meetinghouses . . . in [which] they held . . . religious meetings,
under ministers of their own nation" (pp. 44–45). I suspect that a remark by Zaccheus
Macy (*ibid.,* p. 268) bears on the source of Mather's concern: "Our old Indian na-
tives . . . at their meetings of worship . . . carried on in the form of Presby-
terians, but in one thing imitated the Friends or Quakers, so called: which was to
hold meetings on the first day of the week and on the fifth day of the week."

[4] Barnes and Eldridge.

[5] Metcalf; "possibly the Rev. Joseph Metcalf (H.C. 1703) of Falmouth" (Forbes).

*in the Distress now upon the Nations, to deliver thy Pure wor-
shippers, from the Fears which are now distressing of them.*

1.G.D. Temptations to Apostatize unto the Superstitions of the
Ch. of E. are Likely to grow upon us. I would endeavour in all
faithful and prudent Methods, as effectually as I Can, to fortify
my Flock against these Temptations.

2.G.D. I Would now fit up as many New Shelves, as I have Children; and I would not only Place thereon the Books, which I
design to bequeath unto them out of my Library; but also every
Week to make Some Accession to their Stock of Books, especially from those which either I myself, or their Grandfather,
have published.

3.G.D. Now Winter is Coming on, I would now send some Reliefs, (with my Counsels,) unto my Wife's aged Mother-in-Law.

4.G.D. I have in View, a Design of Cultivating a noble Subject;
and Preparing and Publishing a Discourse concerning the
Threefold *Paradise;* in which much Learning may be Employed,
and much Service may be done. May the glorious Lord Prosper
me in the Undertaking.

(Laid aside; But Resumed and Finished, in the Winter of
the year, 1726.) [6]

5.G.D. I would Set myself to Study the Good of the Students at
the College, in all the Ways I can think of. Especially by bestowing such Books upon them, as may have a Tendency to
season them with Truth and Goodness. But I would more Particularly Endeavour, that the Scandalous and Infamous Custom
of Abusing the Freshmen, may be Extinguished among them.

---

[6] Completed, as this marginal note informs us, but never published. The manuscript, entitled "Tri-Paradisus," is in the Library of the American Antiquarian Society. See Holmes, II, 1121–24 and 1305.

Considering his innumerable activities both literary and otherwise, as well as the
staggering bulk of his various diaries, notebooks, and "Quotidiana," it seems truly
remarkable—yet thoroughly characteristic—that Mather, fourteen years after making the original entry, should bother to plow through his mountain of manuscripts
in order merely to provide this marginal annotation.

20.d 9.m Thursday.

This Day was Kept as a Public Thanksgiving through the Province. I Enjoyed the Assistance of Heaven in the Private and Public Duties of it. I gave Thanks both Privately and Publicly, for the many Favours of God. And Commanded my Children, to Consider the Blessings wherewith God has favoured Each of them, and What Returns they will make unto Him.

6.G.D. There is an Elderly Gentleman, who has been a man of Business and Fashion in the Place; but now in his old Age is reduced unto difficult Circumstances. I would Set forward Motions of Employment and Provision for him; and Project all I Can, that in his old Age he may be more Comfortably Circumstanced. [Mr. $\Sigma^c\epsilon\alpha\phi$] [7]

7.G.D. When I Enjoy Prosperity or Tranquillity for any time together, it will be a needful Point of Wisdom, for me frequently and Studiously to Enquire, *What Point of Decay in Piety may I now fear in myself, which may Provoke the Holy One, to send some New Affliction upon me?* And Mightily to beware of any such Declension.

1.G.D. Let me Mightily warn my Flock, against the Mistakes and Mischiefs of a *Vain Religion*. 'Tis a Point that Mightily needs to be inculcated.

2.G.D. My Little Son *Samuel,* having Met With a Scorch of hot Brass, which keeps him some Days at home, I would not only make it an occasion for Suitable Admonitions of Piety to the Child, but also Employ him in Reading such things as may be of use unto him.

3.G.D. There is a Remote Relation between me, and the Minister of *Concord,* who has also married my Kinswoman.[8] I would

---

[7] Mr. Sheaf. Mr. Forbes suggests that this may have been "Sampson Sheafe, father of Sampson Sheafe, H.C., 1702. Both father and son were merchants."

[8] The Rev. John Whiting (H.C. 1700) was ordained minister at Concord on May 14, 1712. "About the time of his ordination, Mr. Whiting brought to Concord as

improve it, as an Occasion for me, to Suggest from time to time Such things unto him, as may befriend his Usefulness.

4.**G.D.** By Addresses to me, I understand the Grievous Case of many Souls Resolving upon Piety, and proceeding Some way in it, and yet afterwards Relapsing to Wickedness. It is a Case, which by being well handled among the People of God, may Save many Souls from Death. I would with Earnest Supplications to the Glorious Lord for His Assistances, Endeavour it. About this time, with the Help of Heaven, I dispatched a Work of this importance. I Considered, that I was Entrusted with some Small Talents, wherewith I had not Yet glorified my Lord. In my Acquaintance with Natural Curiosities, I was made Capable of Communicating Something that might give an agreeable Entertainment, unto the Ingenious and Inquisitive Students of Nature. Accordingly, I made a Collection of Such Things, and with some Artifice digested them into Thirteen Letters; which I addressed unto Two Eminent members of the *Royal Society;* for them to dispose of them as they shall judge Convenient. This Collection makes a Book of Many Sheets; and I now forward it for *London,* by the Fleet that is quickly Sailing from hence. It is Entitled, **VIII.)** CURIOSA AMERICANA; *Communicated in Letters from* C.M. *to Several Members of the* Royal Society.[9]

My Glorious Lord, Preserve thou this Work, and give it Acceptance among those that it is addressed unto!

5.**G.D.** I am related unto many Societies. I will See whether a Modest Intimation of such a Tendency, may not introduce me

---

his bride Mary, daughter of the Reverend John Cotton (A.B. 1678) of Hampton, New Hampshire" (Sibley, IV, 533).

[9] The first of these letters which make up the initial installment of *Curiosa Americana* is dated November 17, the last, November 29. The first seven are addressed to Dr. John Woodward, F.R.S., Professor of Physic at Gresham College; the concluding six, to Richard Waller, Secretary of the Royal Society. Characteristically, Mather tried to make use of this communication as a means of getting his *Biblia Americana* into print. The letter of November 17, on the apposite subject of "Giants," is taken from this manuscript and consists in considerable part of a description of its merits and a plea for its publication. See Holmes, I, 199–207 and III, 1305.

as a Member to the *Royal Society*.[10] However I would Endeavour to do the Duty of such an one, by Annual Communications, to increase their Treasures.

6.G.D. One of the Ministers in this Town, who has a Large Family, Conflicts with Necessities; I would promote for him Some Supports, and Encouragements.

The Sermon which I delivered yesterday, being filled with *Abridgments,* Exhibiting Still in a *few Words,* [my Text was Heb. 13. 22.] the Illustrious points, both the *Duties* and the *Mysteries,* of Christianity; and it being a real Service unto Piety, for people to Have Such things agreeably abridged unto them, and the *Word Cut short in Righteousness;* I Sent my Sermon this Day unto the Bookseller; that it may be published, under the Title of, GRATA

(IX.) BREVITAS. *An Essay made in a FEW WORDS, to demonstrate, that a Few Words may have much comprised in them. With the most weighty Matters of Religion offered in Several Abridgments, as particular Demonstrations of it.*

7.G.D. I will take a Catalogue of the Books I have Written; and upon Each of them, with a solemn and awful pause, consider to what Special Article of Piety, I should be myself thereby awakened; and accordingly make my most importunate Supplications unto the Lord.

1.G.D. The case of Relapses and Abortions attending a Work of begun Repentance, has in my Flock those Examples, that Cry for me to Speak unto it; I would with the Help of Heaven Endeavour it.

2.G.D. My worthy Friend in *London,* sends me the Lives of Mrs.

[10] Since 1913 historians have generally accepted George Lyman Kittredge's conclusion that Cotton Mather did not take it upon himself to propose his own membership in the Royal Society. Although Professor Kittredge presents an overwhelming array of scholarly documentation, his argument ultimately rests on inferences drawn from documents "not known to be extant" and on a highly debatable interpretation of certain remarks made to the Society by Waller. The entry for November 27 confirms the possibility that the proposal concerning Mather's membership originated neither with Waller nor with Woodward, but with Mather himself ("Cotton Mather's Election into the Royal Society," *Publications of the Colonial Society of Massachusetts,* XIV [1913], 81–114; see especially pp. 84–85).

Terry, and Mrs. *Clissould.*[11] I would Sit with my children, while they read over the Story, Paragraph by Paragraph Alternately; and as they go along I would make Remarks upon Such Passages in the several Paragraphs, as I would have them to take Peculiar Notice of. Lord, Bless this Action!

3.**G.D.** I have a kinsman at *Hampton,* who, I am afraid, is not Good, yet he affects to appear Good, and appears very ready to Do Good: I would make use of him therefore, to Serve the Kingdom of God, in that Neighbourhood, and furnish him with Instruments for that purpose.

4.**G.D.** It being the Time, for dispatching Letters and Packets, to *England,* I would Still, when Writing Each of my Letters, Consider with as Exquisite Contrivance as I Can, What Good Intention, and what Method and Motion to do Good, may be pursued in the Writing of it. I would also propose unto the Booksellers here, the Reprinting of the Lives of the Two Pious Gentlewomen, which I have Lately received from *London.*

5.**G.D.** Among the Commissioners of our Indian affairs, we have so much Encumbrance from the Boisterous, Clamorous and Impertinent Loquacity of One Man, that I am under much Temptation to Leave their Company and write home that my place may be Supplied by another.[12] But I would in this do nothing rashly; and I would call to mind the admirable Example of our Great Saviour, bearing the froward and foolish Humours of His Disciples. However, I would in the Meantime, do my best, that the Indirect Intentions of some, to discourage

[11] The reference is to Thomas Reynolds, *Practical Religion Exemplified in the Lives of Mrs. Mary Terry. . . . And Mrs. Clissould* (London, 1712). A reprint of this work, augmented by Increase Mather's four-page epistle "To the Reader," was published in Boston the following year (Holmes, *Increase Mather, A Bibliography,* no. 156).

[12] Though identification is impossible, one suspects that Mather has in mind fellow "Commissioner" Joseph Dudley. The entry of November 5, 1713, indicates that Mather actually did request his own dismissal: "The Corporation in *London,* having refused to dismiss me (as I desired,) from sitting with the Commissioners for the Evangelical Affairs among the Indians, I would more than ever set myself to serve them" (II, 252).

the English Preachers to the Indians, may be diverted. For, to dishearten them, will be to Ruin all.

6.G.D. One that was more than forty years ago my Schoolmaster, is crippled with much Poverty, but has the thousand times greater unhappiness, of being an ungodly man. I would write unto him; I would Send him some Relief of his Necessities; But I would therewithal as decently, but as pungently as I can, advise him to the Repentance that is Necessary for him, and mention to others, his Necessitous Condition. I now and then also meet in the Street a poor, and a very old, man, whom I knew, to be a man in years, when I was but a child. I would Stop him, and Speak to him about his Preparation for Death, and Put a Book of Piety, into his hand for that purpose. [Πορτερ] [13]

7.G.D. By the Marvelous Providence of God, I am sometimes Entrusted from Unknown Hands, with the Dispensation of Secret Charities. I would make this an Occasion of Three Things. First; of Importunate Cries to Heaven, that I may not after all be a Castaway. Secondly; of being yet, if it be possible, More Liberal in my own Expenses the same way. Thirdly; of Quickening the Objects of these Kindnesses, unto Services for the Kingdom of God. I would also pray for Blessings, on the Unknown Friends, that find this Employment for me. And as I would use all imaginable Fidelity in my Stewardship, so I would use as much Discretion as may be, to avoid misapplication.

6.d 10.m Saturday.

I Set apart this Day for the Fast of the Closet; on Such Occasions as have used heretofore to put me upon the Keeping of such Days in the recurring Seasons for them. And now particularly to pray, that the Papers I am Sending to *London,* may be preserved thither, and accepted there.

[13] Porter.

Dispensing of Alms this day, and Laying aside the Sum of Twenty shillings apiece, for Several Country-Ministers, I wrote the Names of Seven on bits of Paper, who Stood equally fair for the Charity, and then Looking up to Heaven, I drew the Lots, for the Number I intended, which was not Exceeding Four. I am sending the money to them; with Certain Books of Piety; and with agreeable Scriptures [Such as Rev. II. 19. Psal. XXXVII. 3. Matth. VI. 31, 32, 33.] [14] written on the Papers in which the Money is Enclosed.

1.G.D. I am advised, that it may be a seasonable Service, to Preach a Sermon, that shall warn the Young People of the Flock, against the Contempt which too many of them cast on a Religious Education; and Especially in running away to Sea, against the Inclinations of their Parents; But at the Same time, to quicken parents in bestowing a Religious Education, and advise Children how to behave themselves, when they are under the Chastizing Hand of God, for their Sins against it.[15]

7.d 10.m Lords Day.

At the Lords Table, I first celebrated the astonishing Mystery, of the Son of God being delivered up as a Sacrifice for us all; and Put in my Claim for an Interest in that Sacrifice. Then, I made my Humble and Hopeful plea, for All Things to be freely given to me on His Account; Especially, Pardon, Holiness, Fruitfulness, and at Last a Part in the Heavenly City with Exceeding Joy.

2.G.D. Having founded and fixed Separate Libraries for Each of my Children, I would not only be making of Continual Additions thereunto, but also assign Ever now and then Things from thence to be Read by them, and Expect some Account of what they have Read, and on a Good Account give them a Good Reward.

3.G.D. The prayer-hearing Lord, is giving a fresh prospect of a Strange Deliverance for my poor kinswoman, who has been so

[14] Originally in margin.   [15] See p. 100 (Dec. 15).

many years a Captive among the horrible Indians. I would now Renew and Bespeak yet more ardent prayers, that a mercy so near to the Birth may not Miscarry; and assist her nearest Relatives, to do Some Special Thing for the glory of the Great Redeemer, on the Arrival of the occasion.[16]

4.**G.D.** I incline to publish unto the Country, the Sermon, which I am now preparing, for young men, and their Teachers; And with it, the Letter I have received from a gentleman at *Connecticut,* concerning the Remarkable Circumstances of his own Prodigal and Repenting Son. It may do very much Good in the Country.

5.**G.D.** It is time, to put the Societies on their Day of prayer, which they use to have once a year; but was the Last year omitted, by being too Long deferred.

6.**G.D.** There is a Point, which I design to bring very much into my Conversation. When I Converse with people, that are (Especially) under Chronical Maladies, (as, Suppose the Gout,) but are wealthy, or well-accommodated in the world; I would propose unto them, to Look out for some other person under the Like Maladies, but Such an one, as is poor, and Low, and destitute of all Good Accommodations; and Charitably dispense Reliefs unto them; and in this way of Well-doing to bespeak the Mercies of the Lord. I have diverse, more than one or two Instances in my Eyes, at the Writing of this.

7.**G.D.** I find my Soul grievously distempered, with unattentiveness, in the Worship of God; In praying and in Hearing, I am apt to be Criminally unattentive to what I am engaged in. Yea, though I myself am uttering the prayers; When they are Such as I use much of a Form for them. What shall I do for the Cure of this woeful and baneful Distemper? I would affect myself

---

[16] Eunice Williams (1696–c. 1786), daughter of Eunice (Mather) Williams and the Rev. John Williams (H.C. 1683), had been captured (February, 1703/04) in the Indian raid on Deerfield. Taken to Canada she became a convert to Catholicism and married an Indian. In spite of Mather's hopes, she remained faithful to her new religion by steadfastly refusing to be "redeemed." See Sprague, I, 215–17, and Sewall, *Diary,* II, 374 and note.

with the Evil of it; I would Look up to my great Saviour for Help against it; But then I would in a Special Manner Endeavour this way of Awakening a Slothful Soul; When I am going about my Act of Worship, I would Seriously Consider; *This may be [the] Last Time, of my Approaching to the Glorious God in this way, as Long as I Live!*

$$\frac{13.d}{14.d}\ 10.m$$

In the Night, I Spent some Time Extraordinary in Supplications to the Lord. Especially for a Blessing upon one Essay more, which I am now making, to Warn the young People of the Country, against the Paths of the Destroyer. As also, that the Packets I am Now sending to *England,* may be preserved, and find Acceptance. And on other occasions.

But I have Cause to Lie in the Dust, and mourn Exceedingly before the Lord; because I find the Spirit of prayer, methinks, much withdrawn from me. I Converse not with Heaven so familiarly, and with such freedom and such fervour, as I have sometimes done. I must be restless, till I recover a more Intimate Communion with the Heavenly World, and a greater Enlargement of Heart, in approaching to the Throne of Grace. The Sin which Lies at the Bottom of my Desertion, must be found out, and I must get it Pardoned, and Conquered, and Forsaken.

1.G.D. There is much talk, of our Church Swarming into a New Meeting-house, because the Neighbourhood Grows Very Numerous. I would Entertain this matter with all Possible Candor, and Caution, and Humility; Offer no Contradiction to it; Earnestly desire to know the Mind of the Lord Concerning it; Beseech of Him to preserve me from every wrong Step or Word about it; and Cry to Him, that He would graciously overrule the matter so, that none of the Devices of Satan may prevail to hurt Religion, or my Ministry, on this occasion.[17]

[17] "At a Meeting of the Church, Wednesday, 11.d 1.m, 1713. . . . Voted;

2.**G.D.** It would be of Good Consequence, if when I See any of my Children appearing with a New Garment on, I should Put them in mind of Some New Desire, which they may agreeably now mention in their prayers before the Lord.

The Divine Providence, which Wonderfully multiplies my opportunities to Do Good, Orders it, that the Sermon which I preached yesterday, is this Morning urgently Called for, that it may be published. I Consider, that it may Prove of Manifold Use, both to Parents, and Children, in many parts of the Country, to have Such Admonitions Lodged in their hands. I annex unto the Sermon, a Letter which I received from a Gentleman in *Connecticut,* relating the Remarkable Circumstances of his own Son; which gave some occasion unto the Preaching of the Sermon. So I give it unto the Bookseller under this Title: REPEATED WARNINGS. *Another Essay to Warn Young People, against Rebellions that must be Repented of; but unto Repentance, when they have been Rebellious. Or, Serious Advice unto Children to beware of Disobedience unto the voice of their Teachers, and unto them that Should be their Teachers, to do their Duty to them. With a Pathetical Relation of what occurred remarkable, in the Experiences of a Young Man, who made an hopeful End Lately at* Lyme *in* Connecticut.

(X.)

3.**G.D.** The Death of a Relative at *Charlestown,* furnishes me, with an Occasion, to address my surviving Relatives there; Especially the Aged ones; with Admonitions, relating to their own Call out of the world.

Whereas Fourteen of the Brethren in this North Church, have in an Instrument Signed by them, addressed the Church for their Allowance of their Proceeding in an orderly way, which they have in the said Instrument expressed their Intention for,—to the Building of a New Meeting-house, and forming themselves into a Church-state, when things are come to a due Maturity for it. The Church does grant the Request of the said Brethren; Advising therewithal, that for the Circumstances of their Proceeding, and also for the Choice of their Minister, they Endeavour to follow the best Advice, and what may be most for Satisfaction" (Cotton Mather's manuscript, "Records of the Second Church," Vol. IV [1689–1716]).

16.d 10.m Tuesday.

I Spent this Day, with the Societies of Reformation, Who Kept it as a Day of Prayer together. Another Minister Carried on the Services of the Forenoon, I those of the Afternoon; With Gracious Assistances of Heaven.

4.G.D. Among my other Ultramarine Services, I would again transmit unto the Lower *Saxony,* Such things as being translated into High Dutch, may Serve the Kingdom of God, in those Countries; and Particularly Encourage Dr. *Franckius* and his *Orphan-house.*[18]

5.G.D. I may do well, to Convey unto Each of the Religious Societies, One of the printed Letters, concerning the Agreement for a Weekly Hour of Prayer, on behalf of the Church of God; And so, draw as many of them as may be, into the Agreement.[19]

6.G.D. There is a Young Gentleman, a Stranger, who has a Soul Visited with Many Distresses about his Interiour and Eternal State; and greatly needs my best Assistances; which therefore I would afford unto him.

[18] August Hermann Francke (1663–1727), who founded the famous orphanage at Halle, was one of the foremost leaders of the Pietist movement in Germany. According to Kuno Francke ("Cotton Mather and August Hermann Francke," *Harvard Studies and Notes in Philology and Literature,* V [1896], 57) the record of Mather's correspondence with the Pietist leader represents "the earliest expression of sustained interest, on the part of Americans, in German affairs." Mather's interest in "Francke's great philanthropic undertakings . . . [affords] . . . one of the finest instances of that generous enthusiasm and cosmopolitanism which runs through American history" ("Further Documents Concerning Cotton Mather and August Hermann Francke," *Americana Germanica,* Vol. I [1897], no. 4, pp. 31–32).

[19] On December 25, 1712, in a letter to John Winthrop (*MHS,* Series 4, VIII [1868], 413) Mather refers ominously and vaguely to the many evils of the day—"A Day, in which," he asks, "what is to be done?" He adds that "The Enclosed Printed Letter will a little inform you." That this previously unidentified document was "One of the printed Letters" mentioned in the entry for December 18 seems highly probable. See p. 113, n. 32, and the "Printed Letter" on pp. 114–17.

7.G.D. My watch over the Dispositions of my Mind, at the Time when I hear the Sinful Miscarriages of other People mentioned, must be quickened into the greatest Caution imaginable. First, I must be very Cautious, that I do not Rejoice in Iniquity, but be heartily troubled and Sorry, that any Person should fall into any Iniquity. And, Secondly; I must make some Holy Reflection, by way of Warning to myself, and if it may be to others also, Confessing how Easily I should fall into the Like Fault, if Left unto myself; and advising against such things as may Lead unto it.

1.G.D. I renew my Consideration, that it is a point of great Consequence, to be inculcated on my Flock, and will Compendiously obtain those good Ends upon the People, which I most of all Desire to see obtained: For them to be Sensible, that *they have to do with God,* in their Various Exercises and Calamities; and that nothing Ever Can have any power to hurt them, Except it be given from Above.

2.G.D. One Special Action, which I am now doing in relation to my Children, is the Furnishing of their Libraries. Herein I would use the best of my Discretion; and make it a Sweet Occasion of Encouraging them to Read things that may be of the greatest Advantage unto them. One Expedient among others I intend shall be this; When I bestow any New Book on Such of them, as are able to Write, the Condition of their becoming the owners of it, shall be, their first of all Writing out of it, into their blank Book, Such Passages as I shall assign unto them. And they who are not old Enough to write, may Learn Something by Heart.

3.G.D. In this Cold Season, I would Keep a particular Eye on the Health of my Aged Parents; and advise them therein the best that I can.

And whereas, there are many, who are so remotely akin to me, that it must be but a piece of pleasancy to own the Kindred; I would yet Endeavour to Enumerate them, and inasmuch as my Circumstances are so Superiour, that they Will not count themselves dishonoured, in my Claiming of the Kindred, I would Present a Book of Piety to Each of them, and render the Tender of it acceptable, by Letting them know on that occasion, how willing I am, that they should Consider me, as under the obligations of a Kinsman to them.

4.**G.D.** The Impieties of Christmas-Revels are Likely to Prevail among Some of our Young People. My Lecture falling out on the very Day of Christmas, I would make it an opportunity to bear a Testimony against such Impious practices. May the Holy Lord Accept and Prosper the Testimony! [20]

5.**G.D.** There are Services which I would put others upon the doing of. I would write unto some Capable Hands in *England,* that they would give the Public a Martyrology of the English Dissenters. I would write unto Some in *Scotland,* for the Like Performance, on the behalf of their Sufferers. I would Promote a Letter of Thanks from the Ministers here, unto Mr. *Pierce,* for his noble Performance in his Vindication of the Dissenters, addressed in the Latin Tongue, *Ad Fratres Exteros.*[21]

25.d 10.m Thursday.

In the Beginning of this Week, I was much perplexed in my Mind, What Subject I should choose for my Lecture; inasmuch as it fell out upon the *Christmas-Holiday,* and there would probably be among the people, much Notice taken of what I should Say on that Occasion. In my Perplexity, I Cast myself Prostrate on my Study floor; I Cried unto the God of Heaven for Direction; and hoped, that the Angel of [the] Lord, would make Some Impression on my Mind, that should be directing to me. My perplexity

---

[20] See pp. 105–6 (Dec. 31).

[21] Rev. "James Peirce [sic] (1674?–1726), dissenting divine," wrote his *Vindiciae Fratrum Dissentientium in Anglia.* . . . (1710) in reply to the *Defensio Ecclesiae Anglicanae* of William Nicholls. "The work, which is dedicated to the clergy of the church of Scotland, contains a very able digest of nonconformist history and nonconformist argument, marked by acuteness and dignity." *A Vindication of the Dissenters,* an English version, appeared in 1717 (*DNB,* XV, 681–85).

Continued; I fell Asleep; In my Sleep there Came one to me whose *Idea* I Could not remember; and he advised me to preach on, *Ungodly Men turning the Grace of our God into Wantonness.* When I awoke, I revolved the Subject in my Mind, and Soon perceived, how admirably it suited all Good purposes. I Enjoyed a most Gracious and Sensible Assistance of Heaven, in dispatching within a few Hours the preparation of my Sermon. I Enjoyed yet more in the Delivery of it, after that I had in the Dust humbled myself before the Lord. I delivered it unto a Great Assembly; and among the Nine Articles of ungodly wantonizing on the Grace of God, my Last was, That *it is an ungodly Affront unto the Grace of God, for Men to make the Birth of our Holy Saviour, an Encouragement and an Occasion for very unholy Enormities.* On this I Enlarged, and was greatly helped from above, in bearing of my Testimonies.

6.G.D. There are Some Neighbours, who make some Figure in our Church, that are falling into Sinful Contentions;—I would Use the best methods, to prevent their Sin; and Employ influential Friends, to persuade them unto Accommodations.

7.G.D. Whereas my Morning Enquiry, of, *What Good is to be done,* is of so Quick a Dispatch, that it Leaves me Room for many other Thoughts to be also formed, I would Employ the Thoughts of the Morning, as well as those of the Night, more upon the Glories of my admirable Saviour; as they appear, in Each Head, and have relation to Every Truth, in our Holy Religion. And when I Come into my Study, I would insert my Thoughts into the Papers alloted for them, that they may Serve as a Store for me afterwards in my Ministry to Live upon.

1.G.D. In my Catechizing, I would Exquisitely Single out, the Peculiar Vices and Follies, which the Children are in danger of; and Cause a Scripture to be read, relating to Each of those things, and insist on that Scripture with a Vehement Inculcation, and add a pertinent Story, the Memory whereof may be Strong upon them.

2.G.D. It would be a thing of Excellent Consequence, for me to Carry on the *Table-talk* in My Family, with a Yet greater Ingenuity and Fruitfulness. Wherefore I would not only order my Table so as to have all my Children Sitting at it; and at a Stated and Proper Hour; But also, I would there Polish them with all the Rules of Good Behaviour. And I would there Constantly Carry on a Discourse on some Noble and Useful Subjects, which may Entertain the Minds of the Children, and Enrich them with Valuable Notions.

3.G.D. There is a Family in my Neighbourhood, Very remotely akin, to the Relatives of my former wife; but such as Count themselves Gratified in my owning a Kindred. I will take a particular Cognizance of both old and young in the Family; and Endeavour, by my Discourses with them, and by putting Books of Piety into their Hands, to draw them unto all that is Good. [Εδγαρδς] [22]

4.G.D. It may be a Good Service unto the Interests of Piety, on Many Accounts; and Particularly for the discouraging of *Christmas-Revels* in those Parts of the Country, where the Lewder and ruder young People may be disposed unto them, to Publish my Late Lecture, on, *Turning the Grace of God into Wantonness.* And because the Example of the Thief Repenting at the *Last Hour,* has been Singularly abused by the Impenitent Children of Men, it may further Serve the Interests of Piety for me to add a brief Dissertation, wherein I offer Arguments, that he did Repent before his *Last Hour* Came upon him.

Accordingly this Day, I Sent my Late Lecture, unto the Press, augmented with such a Dissertation. It is Entitled, GRACE DEFENDED.

(XI.) *A Censure on the ungodliness by which the Glorious Grace of God is too Commonly abused. A Sermon Preached on the Twenty Fifth Day of December, 1712. Containing Some Seasonable Admonitions of Piety. And Concluded with a brief Dissertation on that Case, Whether the Penitent Thief on the Cross, be an Exam-*

[22] Edwards.

ple of One Repenting at the Last Hour, and on such a Repentance received unto mercy? [23]

5.G.D. When I Send for a Principal Member, in Each of our Religious Societies, which I design Speedily to do, to Come to me together, I would not only Enquire into the Condition of Each Society, and Put them into the way to augment their Numbers; but also Suggest unto them, several Good Employments to be pursued when they are together; Especially, that of Considering the methods to promote Piety in the Neighbourhood.

6.G.D. There is a Gracious and aged Widow, who Lives in a Continual Dependence on Providence moving the Hearts of Good People to Supply her Necessities. I would Supply her, and procure frequent Liberalities from others to her. [Αλλιν] [24]

7.G.D. It is a Point of the Greatest Importance imaginable unto me, that I take heed of *Pride*. There have been Some Singular Favours of God unto me, wherein I have been distinguished from Other Men. The Number of Books I have written. The Methods to do Good, wherein my Life has been Carried on. My Talents not being restrained unto one or two Faculties. These are Especially Three Articles of the Distinction. If I should be proud on these Occasions, it would Provoke the Lord Exceedingly; and woeful would be the Consequences. Wherefore; first, I will Cry to my great Saviour, that I may be Redeemed from this Iniquity. Secondly, I will by much Consideration get it very deeply imprinted in my Mind, what a Nothing, Every Creature is before the Glorious God. And I will, thirdly, Consider Very much on the things which have rendered me un-

---

[23] In this interesting anti-Christmas sermon, Mather demonstrates that the exact date of Christ's nativity is not known and that its celebration is "uninstituted." "The *Day* is concealed; yea, it is now beyond Contestation proved, that not only the *Month* but also the very *Year* of it, has been Egregiously mistaken" (p. 18). "Can you," he asks, "in your *Conscience* think, that our *Holy Saviour* is honoured, by *Mad Mirth*, by long *Eating*, by hard *Drinking*, by lewd *Gaming*, by rude *Revelling*; by a *Mass* fit for none but a *Saturn*, or a *Bacchus*, or the Night of a *Mahometan Ramadam?*" (p. 20).

[24] Allin.

worthy of the Benefits wherewith a Good God has honoured me. Fourthly, I will much affect myself with the View of those Faults and Follies, and abasing Circumstances wherein I have rendered myself more Vile than other men. Fifthly, If a Vain Thought of any Peculiar Excellencies in myself arise in my Mind, I will trouble, immediately Reproach them, Rebuke them, Extinguish them, and Look up to God for the Pardon of them; and be provoked by them immediately to Fly unto some Sensible Acknowledgment of Humiliations attending me, just Contrary to my Supposed Elevations. Lastly. I will beware of being so impertinent, as to take notice in any of my Discourses, of the Things which have been done for me, to render me Singular.

3.d 11.m Saturday.

I Set apart this Day, for Prayers and Alms, with Fasting before the Lord. I bewailed before the Lord, the many Errors of my Life: and humbled myself before Him, Especially for the Pride of my heart. I beheld, believed, received His Pardoning Mercy, and the Mediation of my Saviour Procuring the Application of that Mercy to me. I Cried unto the Lord, for His Favours; and most of all that very much Grace may be given to me; and also for a Good Success of my Ministry; that the Holy Spirit of the Lord would not withdraw from my Ministrations.

1.G.D. It may prove a Service unto the Interests of Piety in the Flock, if I bestow a few written Sermons, on that paragraph of the Gospel, which gives the Relation of the Penitent Thief on the Cross. I also Single out the Principal Sons in my Flock, and Send my Book of *Repeated Warnings,* to them.

4.d 11.m Lords Day.

In the first Action of the Lords-Table, having found first that Impression of Grace on my Heart, which may be called the Circum-

cision of it, and having put away all the Leaven of malice, by En-
tertaining an hearty wish for the welfare of Every man in the
world; I then approached unto my Saviour, as unto the Passover.
I Considered the notable Things in the Jewelitish Passover,
wherein He was Prefigured. And I proposed, that I would Live by
feeding on Him, in the most affectuous Contemplations, until
there should be left a Strong Tincture of Him upon my Soul, and
the Very Temper of my Soul should be to repair unto Him on all
Occasions, and rely on Him for all Benefits, and advance His Kingdom and Interests, and Express a Conformity to His Example. And
having my Soul Sprinkled with His Blood, I hoped for Deliverance
from Destruction.

In the Second Action, I proposed the Death of that particular
Lust, my Pride; and having bewailed the Dispositions of it in my
Soul; especially in affectations of Grandeur, and Inclinations to be
thought Somebody; I applied myself to the Sacrifice of my Saviour,
for the Pardon thereof; and for the purchase of that Glorious
Grace of Humility. I proceeded then, to Consider the Pattern of
my Humble and Lowly Jesus; and aspire after, and resolve upon,
the Imitation of it. And I formed the purposes of a Mind, reconciled unto all possible Humiliations and Annihilations before the
Lord.

2.G.D. A Servant in my Family that appears to be under the Be-
ginnings of Dispositions to Piety, and has never yet been Baptized, is an object that Calls for my Particular Cares, to bring
her on, unto the Service and Baptism of her Saviour. I will do
the best I can for her.

3.G.D. I have a Brother-in-Law at *Charlestown*, whom I may do
well to follow with fresh Instances, upon Certain Points of
Piety, and good Behaviour, proper for him.[25]

4.G.D. I have Many Services of an Extensive Importance for other

---

[25] Possibly John Phillips, Jr., brother of Mather's first wife. If the reference is to
Phillips it is unusually temperate; under normal circumstances Mather considered
him "transcendently wicked."

Places in my Eye. One is, The making a Present of my *Repeated Warnings,* to be Lent in Every Town of *Connecticut.* Another is, The Procuring of a Good Schoolmaster for *Bridgewater,* who may assist and succeed my Excellent Friend [26] in the Ministry there. A third is, for the Ministers of the Town, to Single Out Certain Important Subjects, and Each of us Preach a Lecture on what is assigned unto him, and then together publishing the Same unto the world. Of this, I Will advise with them.

5.G.D. I Would, in the Society, Renew my Proposal, for Some honest and prudent men, to Walk the Streets at the Times and Places, where the children most carry on their Play, and observe their Language and if they find any to use Wicked Language, immediately to threaten them, or use the most proper Methods to Reform them.

6.G.D. A Pious and a Very Aged Widow, that has Lain Long Bedrid, and in the deepest Poverty, requires the Compassions of the Neighbourhood. I make her an Object of Mine, and will bespeak those of the Neighbours for her. [$\Sigma^c a\pi\lambda\epsilon\iota$] [27]

7.G.D. Never, Never would I deal with any person For any Offence, Until I have in the first place very Strictly Examined, how far I may have myself ever have Offended, in any degree of that Point, on which I am to Speak unto my Neighbour; and very deeply humble myself before the Lord, on the Account thereof, and Embrace the Pardon offered with the Blood of my Saviour. And so I will treat the Offender, with that Spirit of Meekness, which becomes one, who himself has also been, or yet may be, Tempted.

1.G.D. That the Devices of Satan may not operate on the Flock,

---

[26] Rev. James Keith (1642–1719), born in Scotland and educated in Aberdeen, was the first minister of Bridgewater, Massachusetts, where he served for fifty years. Keith is mentioned in the *Magnalia* (1702) as one "of such *Ministers,* as came over to *New England* after the Re-establishment of the *Episcopal*-Church-Government in *England,* and the *Persecution,* which then hurricanoed, such as were Nonconformists unto that Establishment" (III, 4).

[27] Shapley.

to which I am related, Especially in the affair of Swarming into another Congregation, I must make more than ordinary Applications unto Heaven.

2.**G.D.** My Poor Son *Increase,* gives me great Cause to Suspect, that he does not yet maintain a Constant Course of Secret Prayer; that he yet Continues too much a Stranger to the Religion of the Closet. I am in Distress on this Occasion. I must make him very Sensible of it. I must Continually, both Charge him, and Examine him how and Where he keeps my Charges. *My God, Pity this Child. Oh! Give a Perfect Heart unto him.*

3.**G.D.** I have a Kinsman, a Physician, at *Windsor,*[28] Whom I may employ in many Good Offices; and I am glad, I find him disposed for the doing of them. I do indeed use him to do good, in all the Towns bordering upon that whereof he is an Inhabitant. But I would Particularly make use of him, to Supply me with such curiosities of Nature, as he may become a Master of; that I may transfer them over to the R. S.

4.**G.D.** Among the English Instructors of the Indians in Christianity, I would Set afoot, a Design of Learning from the Indians, what are their Peculiar Methods in Curing Diseases, and what Peculiar Medicines they have among them; the Knowledge whereof may befriend and oblige mankind abroad in the world.

5.**G.D.** Among the Indian Commissioners, I would Propose, that at our Meetings, we Lay before ourselves, the Account, which the Last Visitation of the Indians, has obtained for us, and at our successive Meetings Consider one paragraph after another, with Projections upon Each Paragraph, for what good may be done among them.

6.**G.D.** There is a Gentleman at *Rhode Island,* who is a Man of Education, and of Ingenuity; but one whose Morals have been

---

[28] Dr. Samuel Mather (H.C. 1698), eldest son of the Rev. Samuel Mather (H.C. 1671) of Windsor, Connecticut, was, according to Sibley, "a famous and busy physician" who frequently served in minor political offices. Elsewhere Cotton Mather refers to him as "an ingenious Man, a gracious Christian, and an excellent Physician" (*Diary,* II, 211).

Extremely corrupted. He has an Esteem for me, and I have some other Advantages to be Useful unto him; Old Age is now also Coming upon him. I would write unto this Gentleman, and Send Certain Books to him, and do the best I can, to bring him unto Repentance. [Πελλαμ] [29]

7.G.D. I must very diligently Look over my Library, and See whether I have no Borrowed Books in it that should have been more Carefully Restored before this time, and faithfully and honestly Restore them. The peace of my Mind, particularly, in Publishing a Discourse about Thefts, and also the welfare of my Library, is concerned in this Action.

The Sermon I Preached the Last Lords-Day, upon the Sin of *Theft*, it seems made an uncommon Impression upon many in the Auditory; and the publication of it by way of the press, is by some Earnestly Called for. I thought a Testimony against the Crime, and a discovery of the many ways, (and some of them, not resented as they ought to be) wherein it is Committed, Might be a Service to the Town and Land. So I did this Week fit the Sermon for the Press, and send it thither. It is Entitled, A FLYING ROLL, *gone forth, to Enter into the House, and Hand of the Thief. The Crime and the Doom of the Thief declared; The Various Ways of his Theft detected; And a Repentance demanded from the Malefactor.*

(XII.)

1.G.D. Perhaps, that Subject, the *Good Man hating Vain Thoughts*, may prove a Copious, a Noble, an Useful Subject, for my Flock to be Entertained Withal.

2.G.D. By Staying abroad in my Visits after nine o'clock at Night, I defraud my Family of many and precious opportunities, which I might have to Communicate Useful Things unto them. Wherefore I would Reform this Error in my Conduct, and Repair home Earlier than formerly, and Spend an Hour, first, in Cultivating the Mind of my Son *Increase*, with all Ornamental Knowledge; Secondly, in teaching my Daughters the Hebrew

---

[29] Pellam. Forbes suggests that this might be Edward Pelham (H.C. 1673) of Newport.

Tongue; Thirdly, in repeating to my Folks, any Valuable thing, which I have read in the Day, Proper for them to be acquainted withal.

3.**G.D.** At *Connecticut,* I have a Kinsman,[30] who is a Physician. I would not only put him on the Exercise of all the Piety, which may belong to a Beloved Physician, but also Sollicit him to Supply me With all the Natural Curiosities as far as he can, that I may make a further Communication of them.

4.**G.D.** A Church being to be quickly gathered at a Neighbouring Town, I would afford them all the Directions and Assistances I Can, that they may proceed comfortably.

The Sin of Promise breaking is grown so notorious, and so much Complained of, that a Sermon against it, at the Lecture, as soon as I can, may be a Seasonable Service.

5.**G.D.** Still as I Come anear the Young Housekeepers in my Neighbourhood, I would advise them and Exhort them, to join themselves unto one or other of the Religious Societies. Thus the Societies may flourish; and the particular persons under the watch thereof be preserved from Temptations and Miscarriages.

6.**G.D.** There are Some Poor Scholars, whom it will be an Act of Charity in me, to assist, With bestowing Such Books upon them, as may much befriend them in the Beginning of a Library, and a Ministry. This is a thing which I desire to take Pains, and be at some Cost about.

7.**G.D.** I Send abundance of Letters, and Packets abroad. As often as I Send any thing unto another, I would form out of the occasion, an agreeable Supplication on the behalf of those to whom I send it. In this way, I would Carry on the Exercise of that Grace of *Love;* and at the Same time Look on Every Visit I make unto Heaven, as a Priviledge and a Dignity.

1.**G.D.** There are Some Things relating to the Good Condition of our Meeting-house, and the accommodation of a Multitude of Hearers, which I would Lay before our Committee, and in all Convenient Methods Prosecute.

[30] Dr. Samuel Mather. See p. 110, n. 28.

2.G.D. My Soul is in Unspeakable Distress, to see the Image of a glorious Christ, formed in the Souls of my Children. What shall I do? What shall I do? to obtain so great a Blessedness? Let this be one among my Many other Methods for it. When I keep a Day of Prayer in my Study, I would Still Call for One or Other of the Children, at some Time in the Day; and after I have discoursed with the Child, I would then pray with him or her, and pour out my Soul unto the Lord in their hearing, for His Grace to be bestowed upon them.

3.G.D. The Books of *Practical Piety Exemplified, in the Lives of Mrs.* Terry *and Mrs.* Clissould,[31] I would Present unto some Gentlewomen, unto whom I am Related.

Since I first began the Practice, I have Constantly Maintained it, of Spending the best Part of an Hour Every Tuesday Morning, Prostrate in the Dust before the Lord, with Cries unto Him, on the behalf of His Church in the Several Parts of the World; Especially our own depraved and betrayed Nation.[32] In this Action, I

[31] See p. 95, n. 11.

[32] A copy, probably unique, of the printed letter reproduced on the next four pages is stitched into the manuscript between the entries for January 27 and 28 (pp. 114–17). The way in which the diaries are stitched indicates that Mather completed his entries for a given year prior to binding the sheets together. What evidence there is, then, indicates that this curious printed document constituted part of the original fascicle. In spite of this fact, Mr. Forbes does not mention its existence.

My efforts to trace the document have been unavailing; but one or two matters are, perhaps, worth pointing out. August 24, the date which appears on it, is just six days subsequent to that of Queen Anne's proclamation for a suspension of arms, which, signed by Bolingbroke and Torcy, was issued on August 18. This clearly is the *"Peace* whereof we have the Plan laid before us" to which the unidentified author refers on his third page—the *"Peace"* which constitutes the reason for the letter's existence. The Proclamation reached Boston on October 24 (cf. Sewall's *Diary* for this date), and on October 29 Mather mentions for the first time hearing of the "Holy Combination" and of the proposal for a special weekly hour of prayer which the printed letter sets forth. Evidently a copy or copies of the letter arrived on the same ship that brought to Boston news of the cessation of hostilities which culminated on March 31 of the following year in the Treaty of Utrecht.

The letter expresses the extreme sense of foreboding felt by nonconformists throughout the period, that ominous sense of imminent disaster that permeates our diary. But fears of a Catholic victory, either in war or in subsequent diplomacy,

have Enjoyed an Unspeakable Communion with Heaven, and a Comfortable Assurance of my being a Member of that Body, whereof my Blessed JESUS is the Head; and it has Left a sweet impression on my Mind, and a Sensible Improvement in Piety, has been the Consequence of it. Sometimes, and very Particularly this Morning, I have had my mind, mightily enlightened, in begging of the Glorious Lord, That He would not utterly and forever Cast off His Poor Creature Man, but Visit Mankind, and by His Holy Spirit Possess, and Enlighten, and Purify Vast Numbers among the Children of Men, and render the World a Watered Garden by mighty Effusions from the River of God upon it. I Plead, that His Kind Intentions towards mankind, have been after an astonishing manner Signalized, in His Uniting a Man unto His own Second Person, advancing a Man unto the Matchless Dignity of the Hypostatical Union. There has also been a Signal, and Wondrous Intimation of those Kind Intentions, in what the Holy Spirit has done for a few, that have been Singled out from the Ruins of [the] Human Race, and been made the Children of God, and beautiful Temples in which He has Chosen to dwell forever. I am filled with Unutterable Groans, for the Day to Come on, when Mankind Shall more generally see and become the Kingdom of God. Some Great Thing is at the Door!

This Morning, I Sang Many Passages of the XVIII Psalm.

4.**G.D.** I foresee a Precious Opportunity to do Good unto Many, in Preparing and Publishing, a Discourse on the Wrongs done to the Glorious JESUS, by People, who are not aware of what

---

are not alone responsible. They are compounded by Mather's belief—a belief which he shared with others—that upon the death of Anne, a Catholic king might be proclaimed in England (cf., for instance, Mather's comment in *The Glorious Throne* after hearing of the accession of George I). But the dissenters had also to fear the "High-Flying Party" whose recent encroachments in Scotland, in the form of increased pressure for Episcopacy and for Anglican ordination, were enough to strike horror into the heart of any loyal descendant of John Cotton and Richard Mather.

For evidence of Mather's concern for "world events" at this time and for more specific identification of those events, see in particular his letters printed in *Diary,* II, 171–77 and in *MHS,* Series 4, VIII (1868), 408–16. For his circulation of copies of the letter, see our p. 101 and n. 19.

SIR,

IT will be a great Satisfaction unto you, to underſtand, That the more Pious and Praying People of God, in the great City of our Iſland, have Entred into an Holy Combination, That they will devote a portion of *Time Extraordinary*, that is to ſay, about an *Hour* more or leſs, once every Week, to be ſpent in the Supplications of the Cloſet, with fervent Addreſſes to the Glorious God, that He would appear for the Deliverance and Enlargement of His Church, in this Day of more than ordinary Diſtreſs now come upon it ; and by His wonderful Appearance, reſcue the Proteſtant Intereſt, that ſeems to Ly bound upon the *Altar*. And very many of them that *Fear God, and can ſpeak one to another*, throughout the *Britiſh* Iſles, are coming into this Brotherly Agreement. We cannot be Inſenſible ; That the Occaſions to *Lift up a Prayer, in this Day of Trouble, and Rebuke, and Blaſphemy*, are ſuch as were never yet ſeen, by us, or by our Fathers before us. What the Famous Martyr made the Concluſion of his Letters, *Pray, Pray, Pray ; never more need than Now* ; is now more than ever, the Concluſion made by all Good Men ; When the Wiſeſt Men in our Iſland, Preach it unto us, That *all Good Men have nothing ſo much to Look after, as to get furniſhed with the Spirit of Martyrdom* ; and we all feel the Fullfilment of what was long ſince foretold by our Saviour, *Diſtreſs of Nations, with perplexity ; Mens Hearts failing them for Fear, and for looking after thoſe things which are Coming on the Earth*. The Chriſtians who agree to this Propoſal, do not thereby Look upon themſelves as Releaſed, from the Remembrance of *Zion*, which they ought to have in their Daily Supplications ; nor would they in one Day *Forget Jeruſal'm*. In this thing they only agree to ſomething over and above ; and they do not lay themſelves under any *Vows* or

Bonds

Bonds, that may Entangle them at all; but referving to them-felves a *Liberty*, to perform or omit, as their Occafions will allow, they only cherilh and follow an *Inclination* to do what they can, of the *Good Thing* that is propofed, But then, there is a further Circumftance of their *Agreement*, againft which, when it is well confidered, I cannot fee how to make any Objection. Our Great Saviour has told us, Mat. xviii. 19. *If Two of you fhall agree on Earth, as touching any thing that they fhall ask, it fhall be done for them, of my Father which is in Heaven.* Upon this Encouragement it is, that the Supplicants of Heaven, lay fome ftrefs on an *Agreement* in point of *Place*; They *Gather together*, and they believe that *Publick* Prayers are præferrible to *Private* Ones : The *Union* and *Harmony* of fuch Prayers is peculiarly grateful to Heaven. But our Chri-ftians can't *come together in one place* for this Glorious Exercife. They therefore inftead of it, have in their view, an Agree-ment in point of *Time*. And the *Time* which they have pitched upon, is, *Every Tuefday Morning, about feven a Clock.* They have no Superftitious Conceit, as if *this Hour* were better than another ; and thofe of them, who are occafionally diverted from *this Hour*, take *another*, to prefent their Petiti-ons to the Infinite Ear, that is always open. But then, they are apprehenfive, that it is in fome Regard, a more *United Cry*, and it will in fome Regard Sound the Louder, in the Ear of the *Lord of Sabaoth*, for being at the *fame Time*, as near as may be. Tis a Teftimony of the more *Agreement* in the Supplications, and by Confequence, it approaches nearer un-to *that*, which our Saviour has encouraged with hopes of Speeding. And it cannot but add fome Flame unto the Devo-tions of a Godly Man, to think, *There are many Thoufands of the Saints of God, at this Time crying to Him, for the fame Fa-vours, that I am now purfuing in my poor Supplications.*

Juft fuch an *Agreement* as this, was many years ago fet a-foot in the *Englifh* Nation ; and fome Divines of Great Re-nown in the Church of God, publifhed Inftruments of Piety, to Excite and Affift the Faithful People of God in the profe-cution of it. The Effects were aftonifhing! There followed Things ever to be wondred at! It is obvious to every Confi-derate Man, that the *Peace* whereof we have the Plan laid be-fore us, Leaves our poor Proteftant Brethren, Languifhing un-der horrible Perfecutions. The ftrength of the Popifh Pow-ers is formidable. The Proteftants every where begin to ap-prehend themfelves on the very brink of Deftruction. Our Divifions here at Home, have a moft formidable Afpect. It is well known, what Expectations are entertained by a vaft Bo-dy of People in our Nations. If all forts of Wickednefs, and a following Infatuation from Heaven upon us, can prepare for terrible Defolations. we feem ready for them. We that are *Diffenters*, were never more expofed unto general Con-tempt, and Hatred, than we are at this Day. We are Loaded with all poffible Indignities; Betrayed by our Friends, and In-fulted by our Enemies; continually trembling to think, what *Cup* our Heavenly Father may further order for us. And what is the worft of all; we have by our Formalities, and Conten-tions, and our *Conformity to this World,* and a fearful Decay of Godlinefs among us, too much ripened our felves for the Judgments of Heaven. We exceedingly need thofe frefh Ef-fufions of the Spirit of Grace upon us, which nothing but a *Vehement Cry* to the God of all Grace, will be likely to obtain for us.

Who can tell, but the *United Prayers* of the Faithful, may be followed with *Voices, and Thundrings and Lightnings, and Earthquakes,* and the found of the *Trumpet,* which will bring on the Time when the *Kingdoms of this World, fhall become the Kingdoms of our Lord?* Prayer will do mighty Things. And the Progrefs of this *Motion for Prayer,* is the only *Good Symp-tome* that in this Day of Clouds and of Thick Darknefs, I can take notice of. Be fure, The Chriftians who come into this Agreement, will take a notable Courfe, for their *own Im-provement* in Piety. The *Hour* which they fet apart for the purpofe now propounded, muft needs Leave an Heavenly Impreffion upon them, and caufe them to Improve towards a *Fulnefs of Goodnefs*. They take a moft prudent Method alfo, to befpeak their own fafety, in an *Evil Day*, if fuch an one muft come upon the Nations, and the *Decree muft bring forth*, and *Mofes* and *Samuel* ftanding before God, cannot prevent it. Thefe, if any, are like to be the *Marked* of God, & his *Hidden* Ones, in that Evil Day. And they will in the mean time, Enjoy the Confolation of an Excellent proof, that they are *Living Members* in that Body of our Glorious Lord, for which they Exprefs now fuch a Lively Concernment. And upon the whole, Tho' Good men may have their Different Sentiments, about fome Circumftances of this Agreement, yet they will all Concur in approving the Defign of it, and Rejoice to hear that the *Spirit of Prayer* is in any manner or meafure awakened among the People of God ; and they will abhor to treat a thing of this Tendency, with fuch *Scorn* and *Scoff*, as it may find among People of a worfe Charaƈter, if they come to be apprifed of it.

All that I have to add, is, That it is probable, the Advice of this matter may reach to fome Godly People, in fome of our *American* Plantations, and it is hoped, they will *join with us*, as far as they judge it convenient. And this the rather becaufe *they* are all bound up with us in the fame *Bundle of Life*, and their Fate is likely to be involved in ours.

I am

Wapping, Aug.
24. 1712.

Sir,

Your hearty Friend & Servant.

they do. If I Live to finish it, I may Enter a further Account of it.[33]

5.G.D. A Body of Christianized Indians at *Sandwich,* is, as I hear, Likely to be destroyed, by a Wicked Fellow, Selling of Rum unto them. I will immediately dispatch a Vehement Letter unto that Neighbourhood, for the Stopping of so great a Mischief.

And I would also Prepare a Circular Letter, unto the Ministers, who have the Care of the Indians, to direct and Excite, their Cares of the Schools under their Inspection.[34]

6.G.D. There is a Poor Man, who has been a forward Professor of Religion, but is now fallen into the Snares of the Bottle. I must, with Discretion and Charity use means for his Recovery.

7.G.D. I am writing a Little Book, about the Establishment of the Law, by the Faith of the Gospel. In the Conclusion of the Book, I give a Demonstration that a Justifying Faith in the Righteousness of our Saviour, is no Enemy to the Law of Holiness, fetched from the Lives of some Justified Believers. I describe some such Believers, in Characters that carry an observable Holiness and Piety in them. And Every Stroke of the Description, I bring out of my own Experience and Conversation. But I would Present it before the Lord, with my Cries, that I may Entirely answer it, and that I may never forget it, never decline from it, never decay in it. And for that purpose also I would with a frequent Perusal Reflect upon it.[35]

---

[33] Published in 1713 under title of *Things To Be More Thought Upon*. See p. 123, n. 40.

[34] See p. 122, n. 39.

[35] See Mather's entries for July 9 and 20, 1712 (pp. 48 and 52). *Adversus Libertinos* appeared in 1713. Concerning this work Mather records in his *Diary* (II, 184) that "from some of the Southern Colonies infested with Antinomian Troublers; I am earnestly cried unto, that I would help them with some Armour against their Errors; and with a Testimony against a Foolish pamphlet spred among the People to disseminate them; and the Concurrence of the other Ministers in this place unto the Testimony." The "pamphlet," entitled *A Spiritual Lawyer*, "Expressly Maintain[ed], *That the Law as a Rule of Life, is no way of Peace; no, not to a Believer.*" Accordingly, it was found by Boston's clergy to be "full of dark, unsafe and unsound Passages"("Preface" to *Adversus Libertinos*).

31.d 11.m Saturday.

I Set apart this Day (as usually) for Prayer with Fasting in Secret before the Lord.

Especially Praying for Direction and Assistance, in Some Special Services, that are now before me.

Particularly, the Preparing and Publishing of some Treatises I have now upon the Anvil.

I Made my Supplications to Heaven for Good News from *England*.

I Cried unto the Lord for the Smiles of Heaven on my Family, and my Ministry, in various Instances.

This Day I arrived unto the Clearest Apprehensions of my Justification before God, by the Righteousness of my Saviour, which I therefore Presented unto Him; and yet my Obligation to Endeavour all Possible Conformity to His Law, in Holy Obedience: the Grace to yield which, the Blood of my Saviour has Purchased for me. I Conversed with the Glorious One, on such Terms as these.

1.G.D. To instruct my Flock mighty clearly in the Methods of their Justification by the obedience of their Saviour; And at the Same time, their own weighty obligations to Love and Prize, and Endeavour all Possible obedience to the Law of the Holy God, and Walk according to that Rule,—And then, to put into their Hands, a Treatise of this Importance,—may be a Service to them.

1.d 12.m Lords Day.

'Tis an Excessive and Unusual Cold, which Embitters the Season this Day. I am forced in the writing of these Lines, to hold my pen unto the Fire, that I may thaw the Ink frozen in it. My Public Services were therefore of an uncommon Brevity.

But at the Table of the Lord, as far as the Time would allow, I Set myself to magnify the Holy Law, of the Glorious God; First, by presenting before God, the obedience of my Saviour to that Law, which has made Expiation for my Violations of it, and brought in Everlasting Righteousness for me; and then, by Pleading the Blood of my Saviour as Purchasing for me the Grace to Love, and Keep the Law; and so taking the Comfort of a Lively Hope, that I shall one Day be brought unto the Perfection of such an inestimable Blessedness.

2.G.D. I would not only Continue my Watchful Endeavours, ever at Lying down and Rising up, Still to Entertain my Consort, with Some New Hint or other, that may [be] Instructive, and help her to improve in Knowledge and in Goodness; But also I would reinvigorate that Law of my Conversation in my Family; whenever I go down among my Little Folks, to Let fall some Expression or other, which it may be useful for them, to think upon; and to do the Like, when any of them are attending on me in my Study. These are indeed no New Points of Care with me; Yet I find it needful to Renew the Charges of God upon my Soul, to observe them, with more of Zealous Industry; and to be more Extensive in my Application of them.

3.G.D. The Death of an aged and honourable Gentlewoman [36] this Morning, who was of the Same Age with my Mother,[37] gives me an opportunity and an obligation to address my Mother with the best insinuations I Can use, to Assist and Quicken her Preparations for the heavenly world.

4.G.D. I am informed, that in the Very populous Town of *Marble-head,* which is near unto us, there is a most grievous want of Household-Religion. Few Families have the Worship of God in them. I would immediately Write unto the Schoolmaster, a Pious and hopeful Person,[38] there, and send him a Number of Books, on that Subject, and Pray him to disperse them, where there may be most occasion and Encouragement.

[36] Mrs. Elizabeth Hutchinson, whose funeral sermon, *Tabitha Rediviva,* Mather preached on the following Sunday.

[37] Maria (Cotton) Mather, then in her seventy-first year, was to survive until April 4, 1714.

[38] John Coit (H.C. 1712).

5.G.D. My Circular Letter to the English Ministers of the Indians, I would have to take in several other points of Consideration, besides what I formerly mentioned for it. Particularly, I would propose to them, the Article of Household-Piety among the Indians,—and the Article of preserving them from those that would oppress them, or defraud them.[39]

6.G.D. I find out another Person [in] my Neighbourhood Miserably Poor; to whom I would frequently dispense Reliefs, in the best way that I can.

7.G.D. Before another Week be Out, I am to begin another Year. Wherefore I would now Look back on the Purposes of this Year, and see, what of them have not been pursued as they should have been, and Quicken my Pursuance of them. And Every way get into the Dispositions of a Poor, Weak, Frail Man, finishing the Fiftieth Year of his Age.

1.G.D. It may serve the Interests of Piety, Especially in the Female Part of the Flock, if I give them a Sermon, on the good works of a Virtuous Woman. Some Such, and One Especially, by Death, Lately departing from us, I have therein a Particular occasion so to do. And I am endeavouring therefore, this Cogent way, to recommend the best Things unto Imitation.

Having Preached a Funeral Sermon, on the Death of an Aged and Worthy Gentlewoman, in our Neighbourhood, I Sent the Copy of it, (and of a great deal, which I had not full Time to deliver,) immediately unto her valuable Son; that he may Publish it, if he please, unto the world. I Proposed herein to blow up the *Zeal of good works,* into a vehement Flame; and very Particularly in the Handmaids of the Lord. The Title of it, is; TABITHA REDIVIVA. *An* **(XIII.)** *Essay, to describe and bespeak the Good Works of a* VIRTUOUS WOMAN, *who therein approves herself a real Disciple of our Holy Saviour. With some Justice done to the Memory of that Religious*

---

[39] In his *Diary* (Feb. 19, 1712), Samuel Sewall remarks, "My Son was very helpful to me in copying out Dr. Mather's Circular Letter" (VI, 371). Mather's entries for Jan. 29 (p. 119) and Feb. 5 (p. 122) prove erroneous Mr. Ford's tentative identification of the "Circular Letter" referred to by Sewall (Ford, *Diary* II, 179, n.).

and Honourable Gentlewoman, Mrs. Elizabeth Hutchinson, *Who Expired,* 3.d 12.m 1712/13, *In the LXXI Year of her Age.*

2.G.D. I would very much Persuade and Assist my Consort, that she may be a Woman full of Good Works.

She shall never want, Wherewithal to Supply her Liberalities.

I will often Renew my Cares, that out of Presents made unto the Family, she may dispense Portions to the Miserable.

I will Put her upon Visiting the Poor and Needy, and such as are in Affliction; and by her hand, send Reliefs unto them; and she shall also Enquire, wherein she may be helpful unto them.

3.G.D. My *Tabitha* being sent unto the Press, I Propose, upon the Publication thereof, to Convey a Book, to the Generality of my Female Relatives.

4.G.D. A Somewhat Surprising Providence Puts me upon Reviewing and Polishing, and Publishing, a Discourse about Unsuspected Injuries which men do unto our Great Saviour, preached near Twenty years ago. I am hereby Supplied, with a precious Opportunity, to write some very pungent Things for the Conviction, both of the Jews, and of the Arians; which I desire with much supplication to Heaven, for assistances, to lay hold upon.[40]

---

[40] The *Diary* entry for March 14, 1712–13 (II, 190–91) provides a full report. "Near nineteen years ago, I preached a Lecture on the Wrongs done to our Saviour, by persons who little Imagine or Consider what they do. A Spirit who with a wondrous Lustre, made his Descent into my Study, declaring himself to be a good Angel of God, and expressing his Desire to have Act. IX. 5. preached upon, was the occasion of my preaching it. . . . A good Man . . . lately asked me for the Notes of that Sermon, that he might repeat it unto a religious Meeting of the Neighbours. Hereupon, it came into my Mind, that I would augment and enrich the Composure, with two considerable Paragraphs; The one, a Conviction of the *Jewish* Infidelity, with the Sum of those Demonstrations, wherewith Christianity triumphs over Judaism; the other, a confutation of the *Arian* Heresies, which are horribly revived at this Day, and the Mystery of the Trinity in God, and the Godhead and Kingdom of our Saviour, opened for the Satisfaction of the Faithful. . . . I give it unto the Bookseller, under this Title; THINGS TO BE MORE THOUGHT UPON."

In this year,

Not One Day has passed me, without forming and Writing, a Contrivance to Do Good.

Not One Day has passed me, without Expending some Little Portion of my Revenues on Pious Uses.

I have not received or given One Visit, without Explicit Essays to Do Good in it.

I have written many Illustrations.

I have sent more than a dozen Books to the Press.

I have Cultivated many Correspondences;—by one Fleet sailing from home this winter, I wrote for *England,* above Thirty Letters.

But, O my God, I Lie down in Confusion before thee. Sloth, and Folly, have devoured an Incredible deal of my Time this year. And the year has been full of grievous Miscarriages.

Desideria Vernalia.

Lord, Let the *Sun of Righteousness* draw near unto me, and Let me be Quickened and Revived, and made a New Creature, and made very Fruitful, by His Benign and Blessed Influences.

Lord, Let a Glorious CHRIST return, Like the *Sun,* to a Miserable World, and bring a *New Face* upon it; Produce upon it a New Creation, and fill it with the Fruits of Righteousness.

Lord, Let the Hours of Darkness grow shorter and Shorter with me.

Lord, Let the Time of the *Singing of Birds* Come on. Let thy Spirit fit me for, and fill me with, the Songs of the Re-

deemed. And Let the Songs of Piety replenish the whole
Earth with an Heavenly Melody.

Lord, Enable me with diligence to Prosecute a Divine *Husbandry,*
and with Patience to wait for a *Good Harvest* of my Endeavours to serve the Kingdom of God. Oh! Let *Light* and
Joy, be sown for me!

Desideria Æstivalia.

Lord, Let me be as Fruitful as any of the *Trees* or *Fields,* which
now Yield a grateful Spectacle. Oh, Let me abound in the
Fruits of Righteousness.

Lord, Let my dear JESUS be to me, as the shadow of a Great Rock
in a Weary Land; And may I also Drink of what flows from
that wonderful Rock!

Lord, Let me be Entitled to, and Prepared for, the Blessedness of
that world, in which no Uneasy Heat will molest thy Children.

Desideria Autumnalia.

Lord, Let me see a *Joyful Harvest* of all my poor Endeavours to
glorify thee. Let me Reap with Joy!

Lord, Let me arrive to my *Grave,* and thy *Floor,* as a shock of *Corn
fully ripe,* in the Season thereof.

Lord, Affect me, and the rest of Mankind, with a sense of our own
Mortality. For we *all Fade* as a *Leaf!* [41]

[41] Towards the end of his *The Life and Times of Cotton Mather* (Boston, 1892),
Abijah P. Marvin introduces a version of these *"Desideria,"* which he has carefully
reserved as in some respects climactic, by observing: "We have seen . . . Mather's
delight in the beauties of natural scenery. . . . But we have a more distinct expression in a passage [in which] the reader will observe that nature led him up to
nature's God" (p. 546).

Mather's parallel supplications or "Desires" for winter appear as *"Supplicationes
Hyemalis"* in the entry for January 19, 1711–12 (II, 152).

The Course of My Public Ministry.

1711

17.d 12.m	I Preached on Eccl.5.7. a *Multitude of Dreams,* wherewith Vain Men, express and support their *Vanities.*
21.d 12.m Thursday.	I Preached, the Lecture, on Jer.13.23. about *Evil Customs.*—Warning the People against Embracing and Indulging of them.
24.d 12.m	I Preached on Matth.13.25. *The Sinful Sleep,* which the Children of Men, Yea, the Servants of God, are Subject to.

1712

2.d 1.m	I Preached on, Matth.13.25. *Hypocrites* in the Visible Church. [And I administered the Eucharist.]
9.d 1.m	I finished, what I began the Last Lords-Day, and pressed with much Solemnity and Vehemency, the Exhortation, To beware of *Hypocrisy;* and gave Notes of *Hypocrisy,* and of *Sincerity.*
13.d 1.m Thursday.	A General Fast. I Preached on Psal.79.9. The God *of Salvation* helping and Saving a Sinful People, for the *Glory of His Name,* notwithstanding their Sinfulness and Unworthiness.
16.d 1.m	I Preached, on I Chron.29.19. The Grace of a *Perfect Heart,* making Blessed Children, and the Concern of Parents, to Pray for such a Blessing on their Children.

20.d 1.m **Thursday.** I Preached the Lecture, to a Very great Assembly, and with a Very great Assistance; on, 2. Joh.4. the Joy of seeing our Children *Walk in Truth*. And I bore my Testimonies, against some Wrong Steps, taken by too many of our Children.

23.d 1.m I Preached on Matth.13.25. ungodly People in the Visible Church, Compared unto *Tares*.

30.d 1.m I Preached on Job.5.1. The Encouragement of Good Men in Affliction, when they see other Good Men in Afflictive Cases which are Like to theirs. With an Admonition, that in our *Graces* as well as our *Cases*, We may answer the *Saints* whom we may turn unto.

6.d 2.m I Preached on, Matth.13.26. the Sincere Christian, a *Growing* one, and a *Fruitful* one.

13.d 2.m I Preached, on Luk.21.36. The Methods of Piety to be taken when sad Changes and Evils are Looked for, that we may be accounted worthy to Escape the Evils.

17.d 2.m **Thursday.** I Preached the Lecture, on I. Joh.2.18. The Notice we ought to take of the Time; Especially, if it have any Symptoms of the *Last-Time*. And Endeavoured to awaken the Country into a Sense of *this Time*.

20.d 2.m I Preached on Matth.13.26. Wicked Hypocrites, and they who Carry on a trade of Secret Wickedness, discovered sometimes in *this World*.

27.d 2.m I Preached on Matth.13.27. *Degeneracy* (the Growth of Tares) in Churches, not only woeful, but wonderful. [And I administered the Eucharist.]

4.d 3.m	I Preached, on Zech.2.4. Important Things, which the Great God orders to be Spoken unto *young persons.*
11.d 3.m	I Preached, on Psal.55.22. The *Burdens* we have to Cast upon the Lord, and the Methods of Casting them there.
15.d 3.m Thursday.	I Preached the Lecture, on Psal.51.18. Offering my Advice, that the *Building* of the Town may be so carried on, as that God may be acknowledged and glorified in it. (The People of the Town being deeply engaged, in Rebuilding their waste places.) [42]
18.d 3.m	I Preached on Matth.13.28. *Satan,* an *Enemy;*—to whom, and in what.
25.d 3.m	I Preached on Psal.147.11. *Hope in the Mercy of God,* joined with a Fear of this Merciful God.
1.d 4.m	I Preached on Matth.13.28. the Servants of God, sincerely desirous to *Know,* and to *Do* His Will.
8.d 4.m	I Preached on Psal.147.11. and finished what I began, a Fortnight ago.
12.d 4.m Thursday.	I Preached the Lecture, on Psal.110.7.— and Concluded with Comforting the People of God, against the Fears of the *Torrents,* which now threaten the world.
15.d 4.m	I Preached on Matth.13.29. the Tenderness of the Lord for His Faithful People; Other People faring the better for the

---

[42] On April 22, Sewall wrote to Jeremiah Dummer in the following terms: "Though it be something with latest (annus abit) yet 'tis more easy asking your Condolence of our Losses by the October fire, now we have the pleasure of seeing persons begin to build the waste-places, especially those of public concern, the Court-House; **and** Meeting-House" (*Letter-Book,* I, 422).

People of God; and Spared, that so they may themselves have a Space to become the people of God.

22.d 4.m   I Preached on Rom.12.10. the Kind Affections and Expressions of *Brotherly Love.* Our Flock discovering many ways much want thereof. [And I administered the Eucharist.]

29.d 4.m   I Preached on Matth.13.30. *Good* and *Bad* People being together in the world, and growing more what they are.

6.d 5.m   I Preached on Joh.6.27. the Evil of Inordinate Labour, for the Perishing Enjoyments of this Life; And the Good Effect of Labouring most for the Eternal Blessedness, which a Glorious Christ Will feed us withal.

10.d 5.m Thursday.   I Preached the Lecture, to a very great Assembly, and with a very great Assistance, on Prov.13.15. the ways of Transgression, *Hard* ways. And I warned the Young People of the Town against the Ways of Dishonesty. [On the Occasion of a Knott of Young Thieves discovered.]

13.d 5.m   I Preached both Parts of the Day because of my Father's falling into a Sudden Indisposition. A.M. on Col.2.13. the *Quickening* Whereof Believers once Dead in Sins, have Experience. P.M. on Matth.13.30. the *End* which the Day of Judgment will bring on the world, and the *Harvest* men shall then see of all their Actions in the *world.*

20.d 5.m   I Preached on Job.22.15. *Remarkable* Things in the Way of Wicked men.

22.d 5.m Tuesday.	I Preached at *Natick;* to the Indians on, Act.26.18.
27.d 5.m	I Preached at the Castle; A.M. on Prov. 18.10. about the repairing to the Name of the Lord, as a *Strong Castle.* P.M. on Job.4.21. the Danger of *Dying without Wisdom.*
3.d 6.m	I Preached on Prov.18.3. the Case of Wicked Men, to have *Contempt* Cast upon them, and the Crime of Wicked Men, to Cast *Contempt* upon all that is good.
7.d 6.m Thursday.	I Preached, the Lecture, on Rev.7.16. a Time to Come, in which no Distressing *Heat,* will be Complained of. [The Weather being Extremely Hot, I took occasion from the *Heat* of the Season, to recommend Christ and Heaven.]
10.d 6.m	I Preached on Matth.13.30. the *Angels* employed in many Services for our glorious Lord; and Particularly as reapers in *Gathering* and *Bundling* the Wicked, at the Day of Judgment.
13.d 6.m Wednesday.	I Preached at *Charlestown,* on a Day of Prayer kept by the people there, in order to their Inviting another Minister. On, Amos. 8.11. a *Famine* of Hearing the word of God.
17.d 6.m	I Preached on Joh.6.34. Christ the *Food* of Souls, and *Bread* of Heaven; how to be fed upon; and how we are to Express our Desires to feed upon him. [And I administered the Eucharist.]
24.d 6.m	I Preached on Matth.13.30. the *Burning* of the *Tares;* the terrible Punishment of the Wicked in another world.

27.d 6.m Wednesday.	I Preached the Lecture at *Dedham;* on Psal.55.22.—how to Cast our *Burdens* on the Lord.
31.d 6.m	I Preached, on Matth.13.30. the Gathering of the *Wheat* into the *Barn;* the Blessedness of the Children of God, in the Heavenly World. My Seventeenth, and Finishing Sermon, on the Parable of the *Tares.*
4.d 7.m Thursday.	I Preached the Lecture, on I. Cor.15.4. the Demonstrations of a *Risen Jesus,* To Confound Infidelity.
7.d 7.m	I Preached, at *Salem,* A.M. on Psal.55.22.—how to Cast our *Burdens* on the Lord. P.M. on Psal.76.2. the *Tabernacle* of the glorious Lord at *Salem;* the Happiness of such a Town, and how to obtain the Happiness.
14.d 7.m	I Preached on, Psal.26.4. who are *vain persons,* and what is the Evil of *Sitting with them.*
21.d 7.m	I Preached, on Psal.19.7. the *Perfection* in the Word of God, and the *Conversion* of the Souls whereof that word is the Instrument.
28.d 7.m	I Preached, on Ps.19.7. and Concluded the Discourse, I began the Last Lords-Day. With Great Flame pursuing the *Conversion* of the Souls in the Auditory.
2.d 8.m Thursday.	I Preached the Lecture, on Lev.26.11. the Happiness of a Town, in which the Glorious One Will Please to have His *Tabernacle.* It being this Day Twelvemonth, that much of the Town was Laid in Ashes; I thought, advice to prevent more such Desolations, might be seasonable.

5.d 8.m	I Preached, on Ps.19.7. the *Sure Testimony* of God, in and with His *Word;* and the *Simple Made Wise* by it.
12.d 8.m	I Preached, on Gal.4.6. the Spirit of God, Enabling His People to Cry unto Him, *Abba, Father;* the Meaning and Method of doing so. [And I administered the Eucharist.]
15.d 8.m Wednesday.	I Preached the Lecture, at *Woburn* on Psal.55.22.
19.d 8.m	I Preached, on Psal.19.8. the *Right Statutes* of God, *Rejoicing the Heart.*
21.d 8.m Tuesday.	I Preached at *Newtown,* on Isa.45.19.— it being a Day of Prayer there, for the Choice of a Minister.
26.d 8.m	I Preached on Psal.19.8. the pure *Commandment* of God *Enlightening the Eyes.*
30.d 8.m Thursday.	A Grievous, Rainy, Stormy Day. I Preached the Lecture, on Luk.21.36. because 'tis Likely to be yet a More Stormy Time in the world. How to become worthy to Escape the Changes and Evils Coming on the world.
2.d 9.m	I Preached on, Psal.19.9. the *Word* of God instructing us in the *Fear* of God; both *Clean,* and both *Enduring forever.*
9.d 9.m	I Preached, on Psal.19.9. the *Truth* in the Word of God, which does advise us of His *Judgments,* and the *Justice* of those *Judgments.*
16.d 9.m	I Preached on, Dan.5.23. who they are that refuse to *Glorify God.*
20.d 9.m Thursday.	A Day of Thanksgiving through the Province. I Preached on Dan.5.23. the *Judgments* whereto they are obnoxious, that

refuse to Glorify God; And how we are to Glorify Him.

23.d 9.m   I Preached on, Jam.2.26. a *Vain Religion*.[43]

---

[43] Although there is no evidence of damage to the manuscript, "The Course of [Mather's] Public Ministry" breaks off at this point.

Index

Index

THE DIARY OF COTTON MATHER

was composed, printed, and bound by
Vail-Ballou Press, Inc.,
Binghamton, New York.
The types used
are Linotype and Monotype Baskerville.
The paper is Warren's Old Style Antique Wove
made by the S. D. Warren Company,
Boston, Massachusetts.
The book was designed by
John J. Walklet, Jr.

0